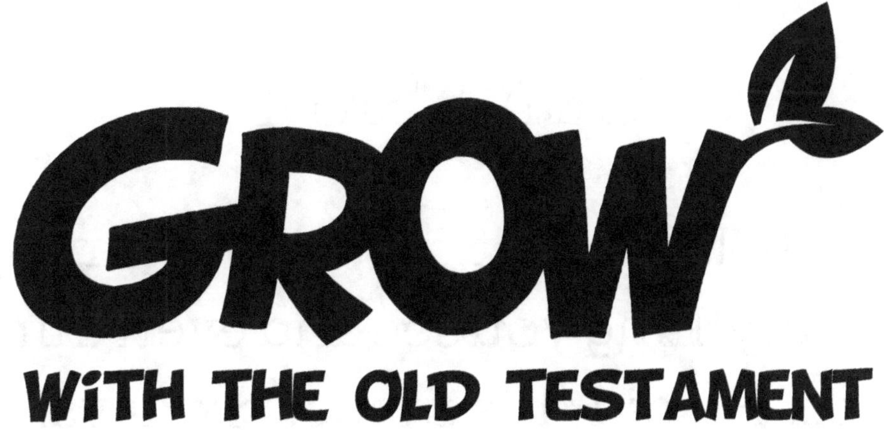

GROW WITH THE OLD TESTAMENT

STORIES BY MICHAEL WHITWORTH
ILLUSTRATIONS BY JASON HUTTON

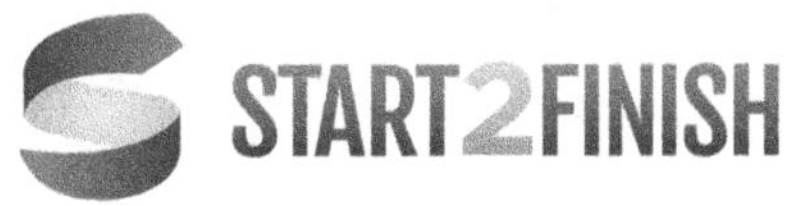

CREATION: DAYS 1-3

GENESIS 1

The Bible tells us that in the beginning, God created everything you see and even things you do not see. He did this in just six days! On day one, God said, "Let there be light." He saw that the light was good. He then separated the light He made from the darkness and called them day and night. On day two, God created the sky and saw that this was a good thing, too. On day three, God said, "Let the waters be gathered together." When this happened, land appeared! Then God created all of the plants, trees, fruits, and vegetables on the land. God thought this was good too, and called the land earth and the waters the sea.

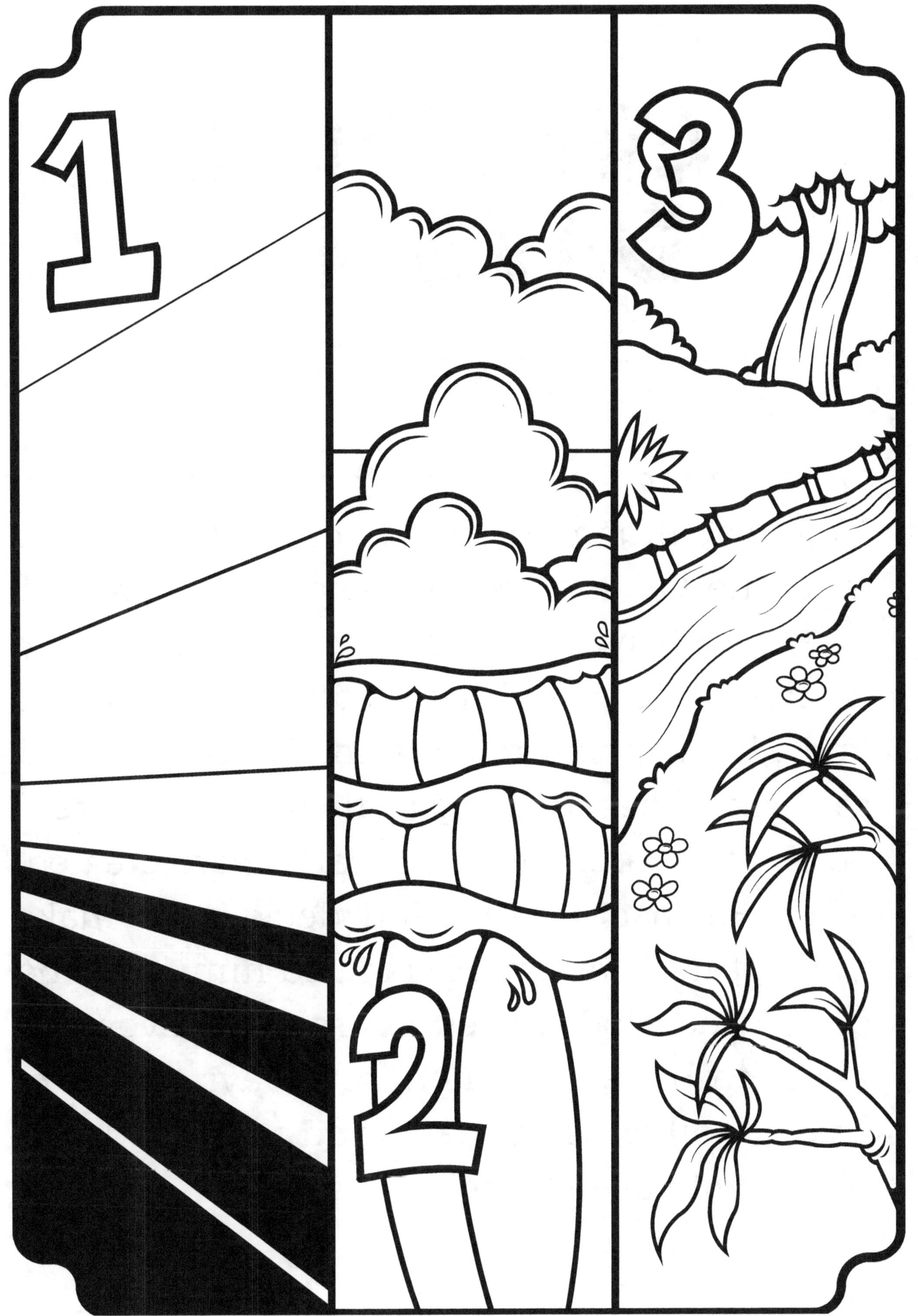

1
2
3

CREATION: DAYS 4-6

GENESIS 1

On day four, God created the sun and moon. He created them to keep track of the seasons and time. On day five, God said, "Let the waters swarm with living creatures and let the birds fly in the air." So everything that lives in the water and all the birds were created. On day six, God said, "Let the earth bring forth living creatures." So all of the animals of the earth were created. After He made them, God decided to make the first man, Adam. He created him from the dust. Then, God created Adam's wife Eve from Adam's rib and told them to always take care of each other as husband and wife. God was happy with everything He created.

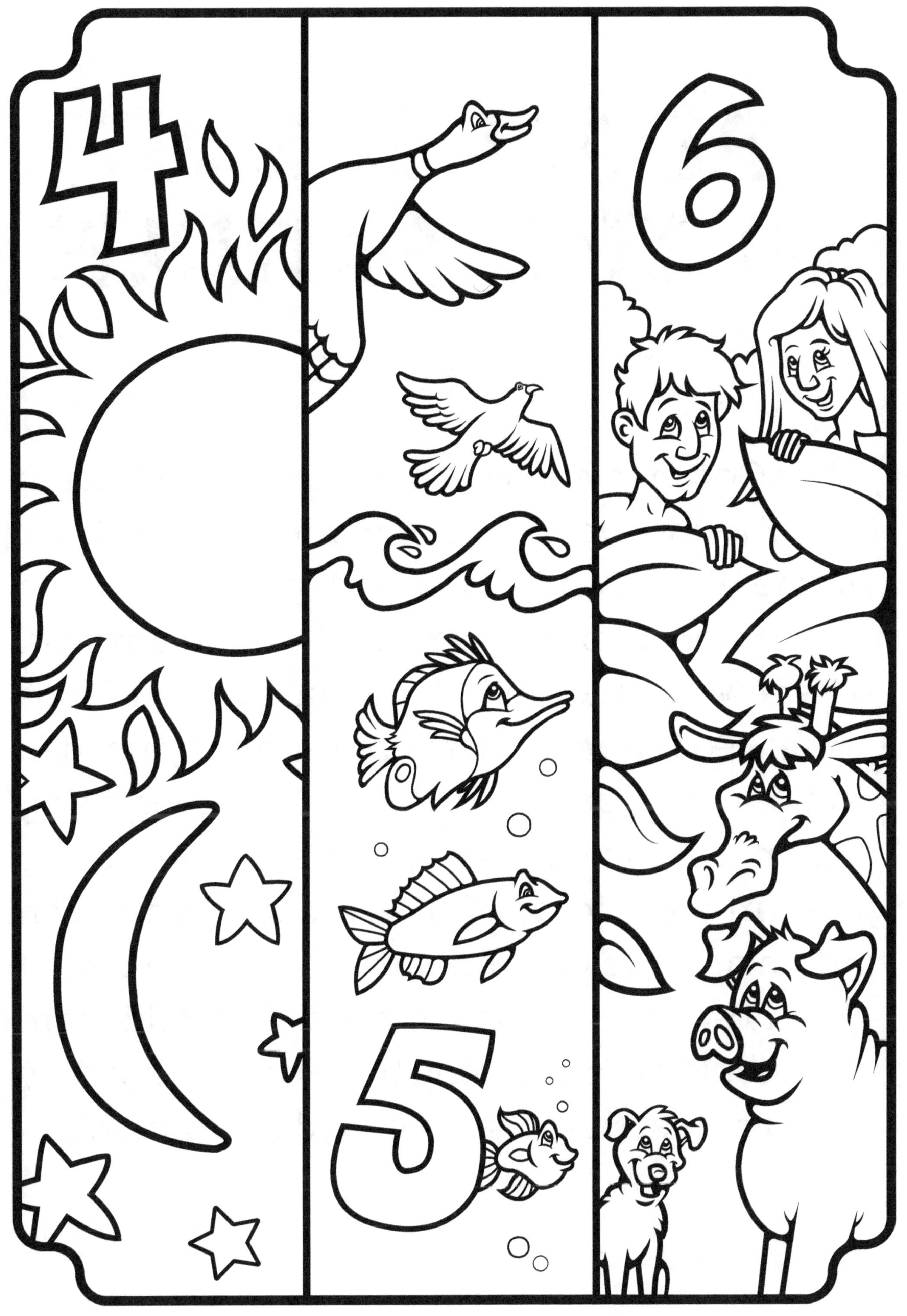

ADAM & EVE IN THE GARDEN

GENESIS 2

After God created everything, He placed Adam and Eve in a very special garden called Eden, where they could live. God gave them the special job of taking care of all of the animals. There were trees and plants full of good foods to eat. God gave them everything they needed to survive. He gave all of the animals everything they needed to survive, too. There was one tree right in the middle of the garden from which Adam and Eve could not eat. It was the tree of the knowledge of good and evil. God told them they could have anything they wanted, but they could not eat from that tree. God was protecting Adam and Eve.

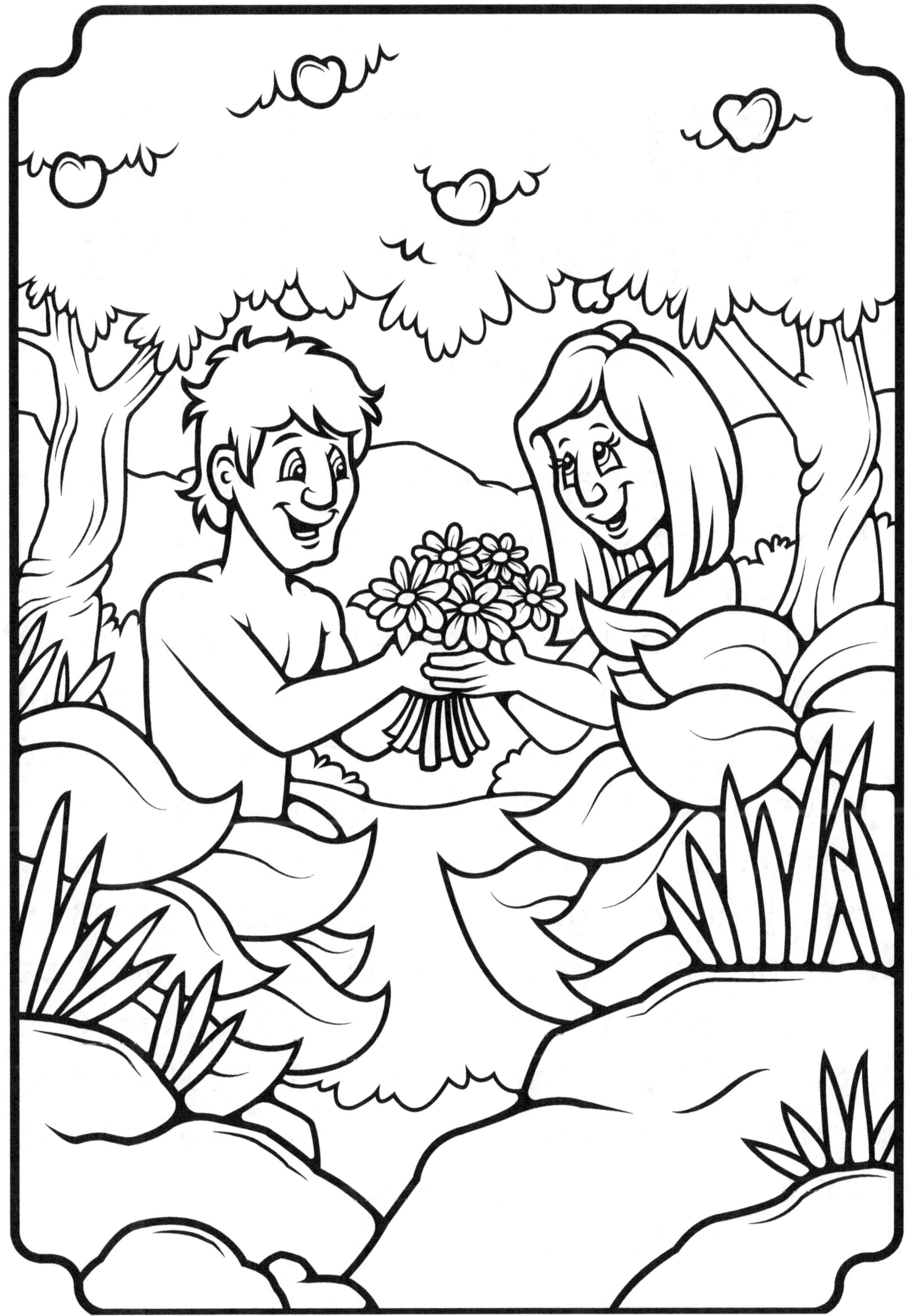

ADAM & EVE DISOBEY GOD

GENESIS 3

God told Adam and Eve they could eat anything they wanted, but they had to leave one tree alone. One day, the serpent told Eve she should eat the forbidden fruit. She decided to eat it and gave some to Adam, and he ate it too! The serpent tricked Adam and Eve because he wanted them to get into trouble! When God came looking for them, they were afraid. They knew they had done wrong. They tried to hide from God. Because they disobeyed God, they had to leave the beautiful garden God made for them. God still loved them and even made clothes for Adam and Eve to protect them because they were no longer in the perfect garden.

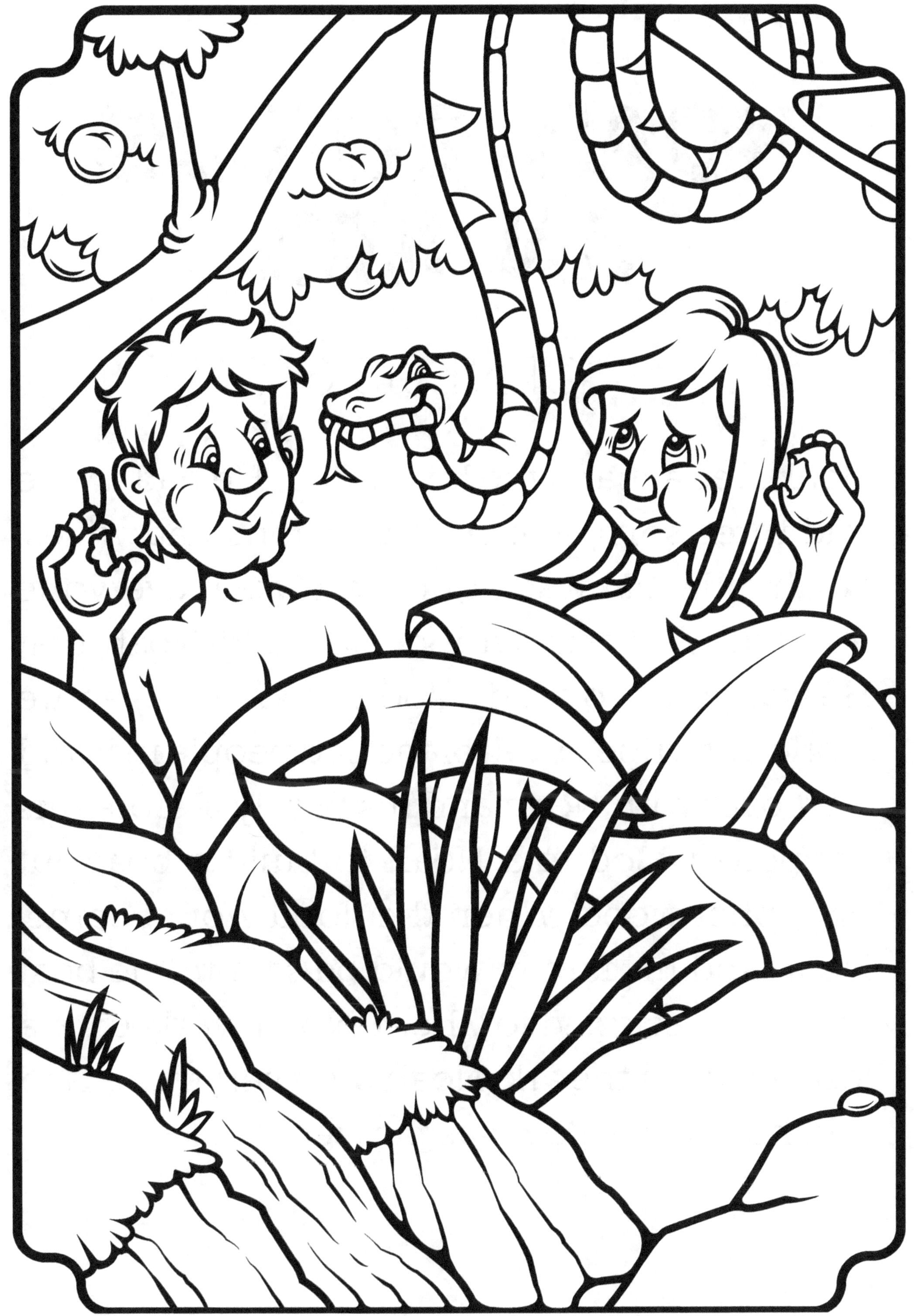

NOAH BUILDS AN ARK

GENESIS 6

Noah was a man who loved God. He had a wife and three sons, and his three sons had wives. Noah did what was right even when everyone else did what was wrong. God told Noah that He was going to send a flood to cover the entire world and wipe out all of the bad people in it and start over with Noah and his family. Before this happened, God told Noah to build a boat out of gopher wood. When the flood would come, Noah and his family would be safe in the boat that God designed for them. Noah worked for a long time on the ark. Noah did everything God told him to do. God was pleased.

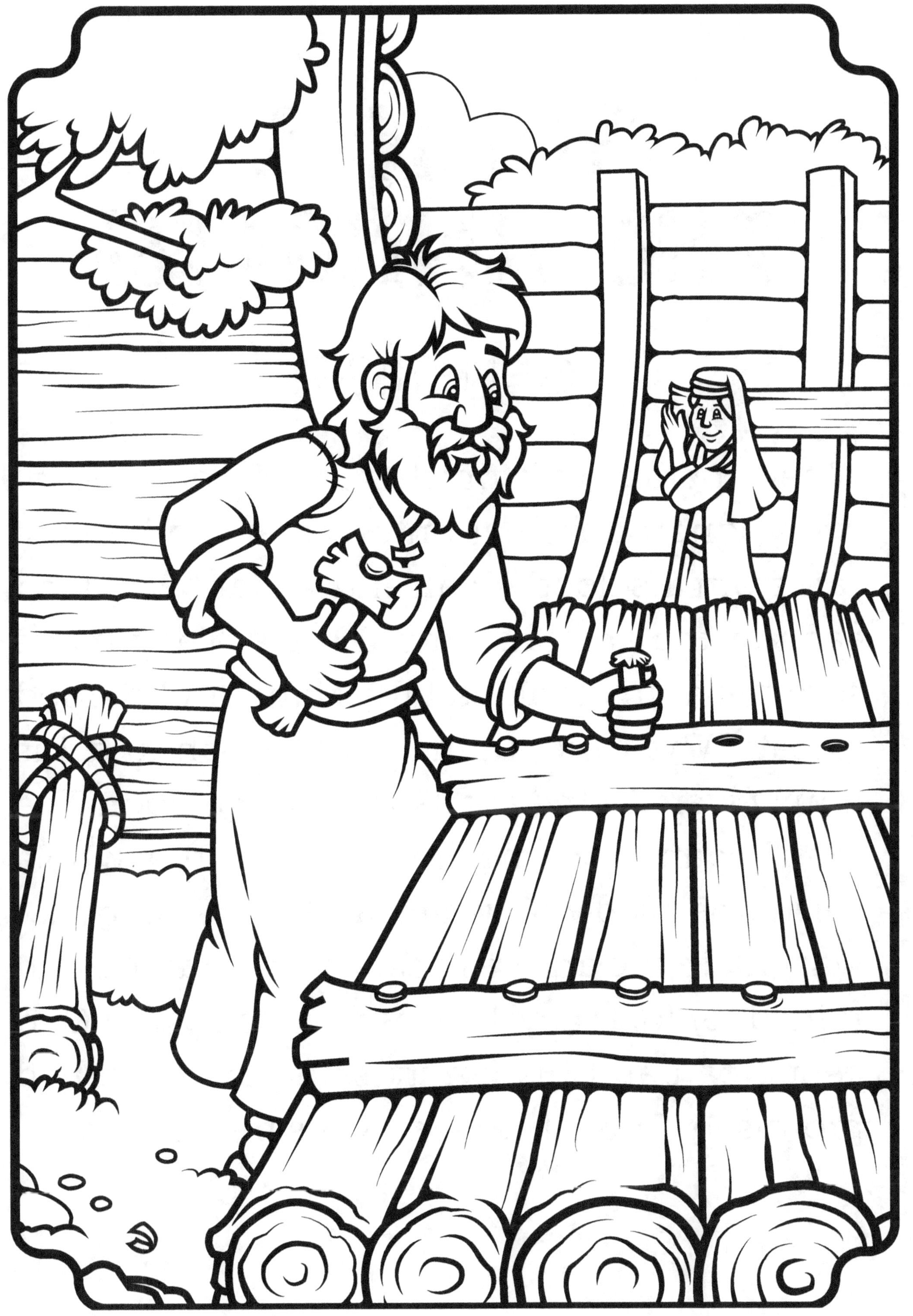

NOAH & THE ANIMALS

GENESIS 7

When the ark was finished, God sent two of every kind of animal onto the ark to be kept safe from the flood. Noah and his family helped each of the animals onto the ark. They made sure the animals all had the right kind of food to eat. When the animals and Noah and his family were in the ark, God shut the door. The rain began to come down. Soon the whole earth was filled with water, and everything that was not in the ark was destroyed. It rained and rained for forty days! It was very scary, but God kept Noah and his family safe just as he had promised. God takes care of His people.

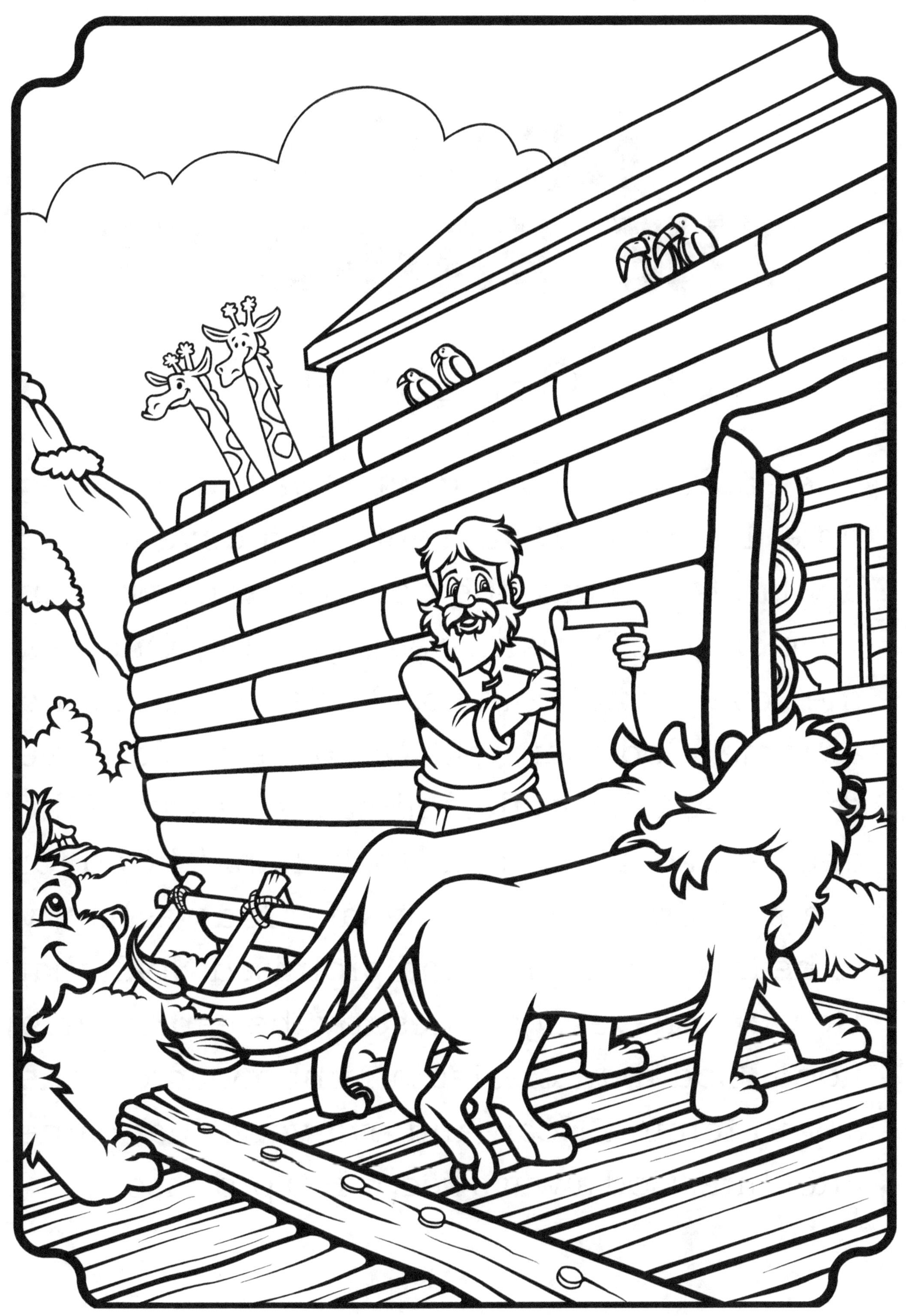

NOAH & THE RAINBOW

GENESIS 9

The earth was covered with water for a long time. Each day, Noah sent out a dove to find dry land. One day, the dove returned with an olive branch. Dry land was appearing! One day, the dove did not come back at all. It had found a home! God then told Noah he could leave the ark! After all of the animals were out of the ark, Noah built an altar. Noah thanked God for keeping him and his family safe. God was happy to hear Noah praying and promised Noah that He would never again destroy the earth with a flood. God then created a rainbow across the sky to remind Noah and everyone that came after him. God always keeps His promises.

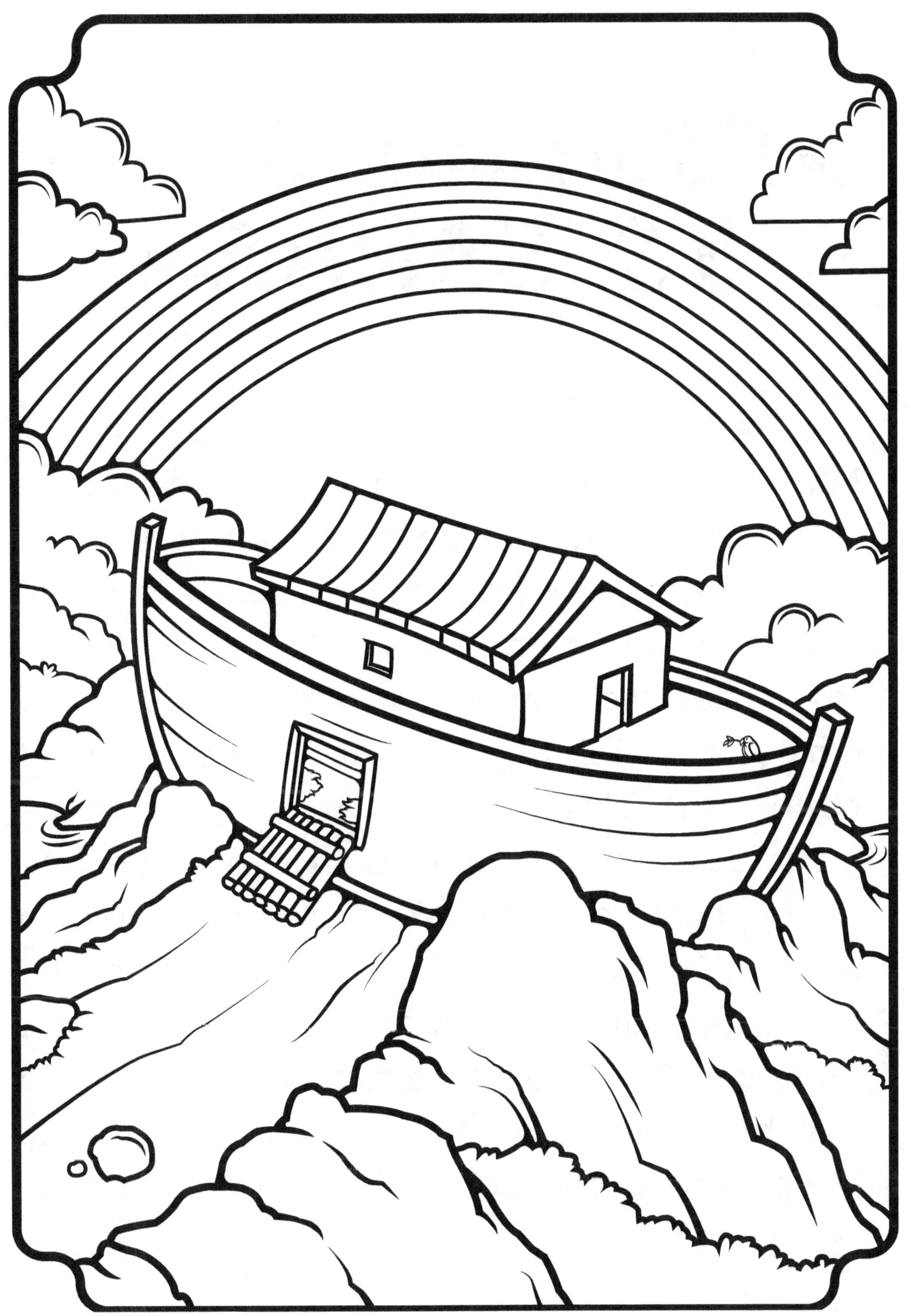

ABRAHAM GOES TO CANAAN

GENESIS 12

Many years after the flood, God chose a man named Abraham to become the father of many nations. Abraham and his wife Sarah were old and had no children. God said to him, "Go away from your home and your father's house to a land that I will show you. I will make you a great nation and bless you and make your name great." Abraham obeyed God. He, his wife, and his nephew Lot packed their possessions and traveled to the land of Canaan. God promised he would later give Canaan to Abraham's offspring. There, Abraham built an altar and worshiped God. Abraham trusted God to keep His promises, and God took care of Abraham.

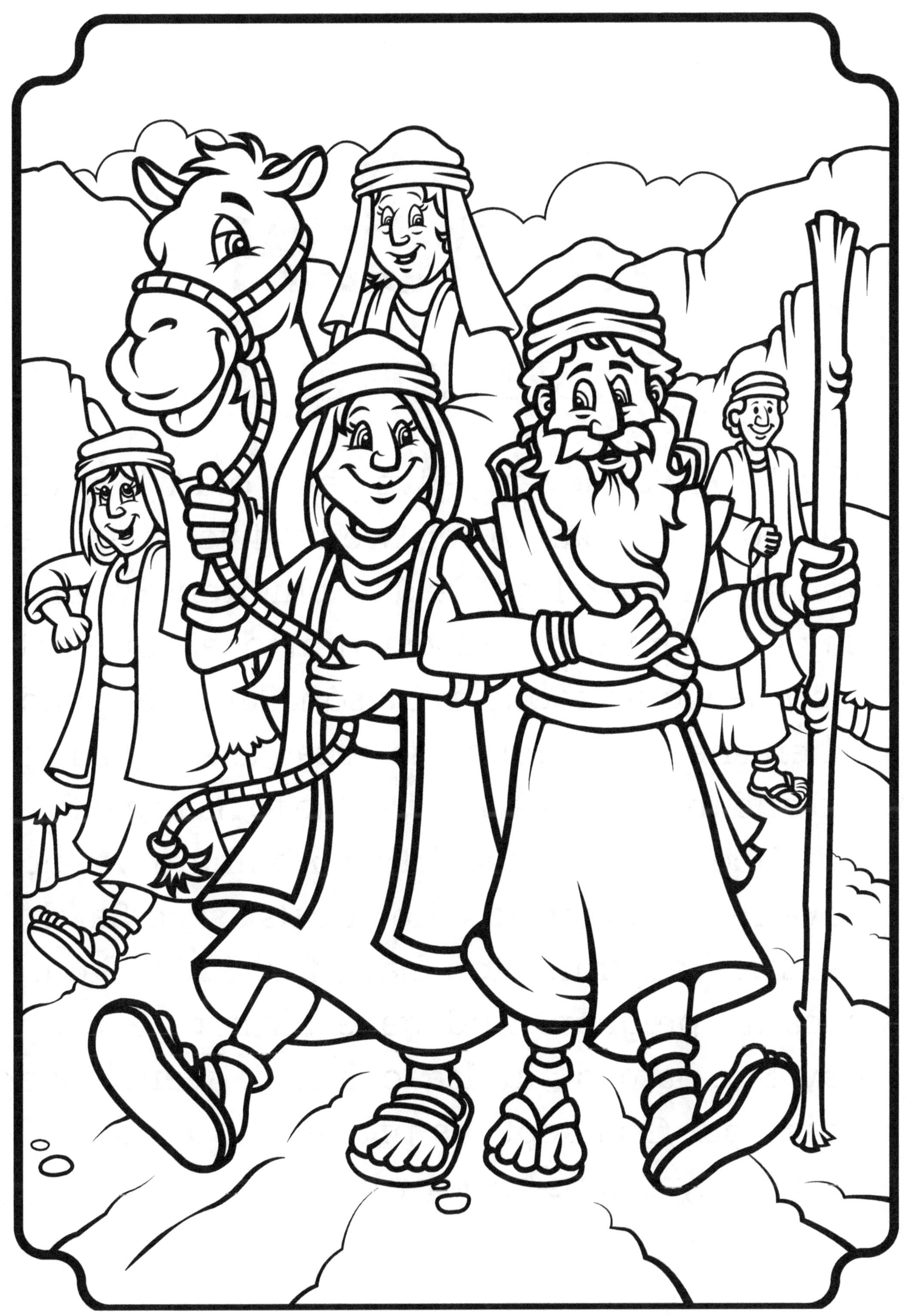

ISAAC IS BORN

GENESIS 21

Abraham was seventy-five years old when he moved to Canaan. After twenty-five years, he and his wife Sarah still had no children. But one day, God sent angels to visit him to tell him that his wife would soon have a son. Sarah laughed when she heard the news because she was so old and thought she wasn't able to have a baby. But God had promised that Abraham would have many offspring. The angels asked Sarah, "Is there anything too hard for God?" Sarah became pregnant and gave birth to a baby boy. She named him Isaac. It took twenty-five years, but God kept his promise to Abraham. God always keeps his promises.

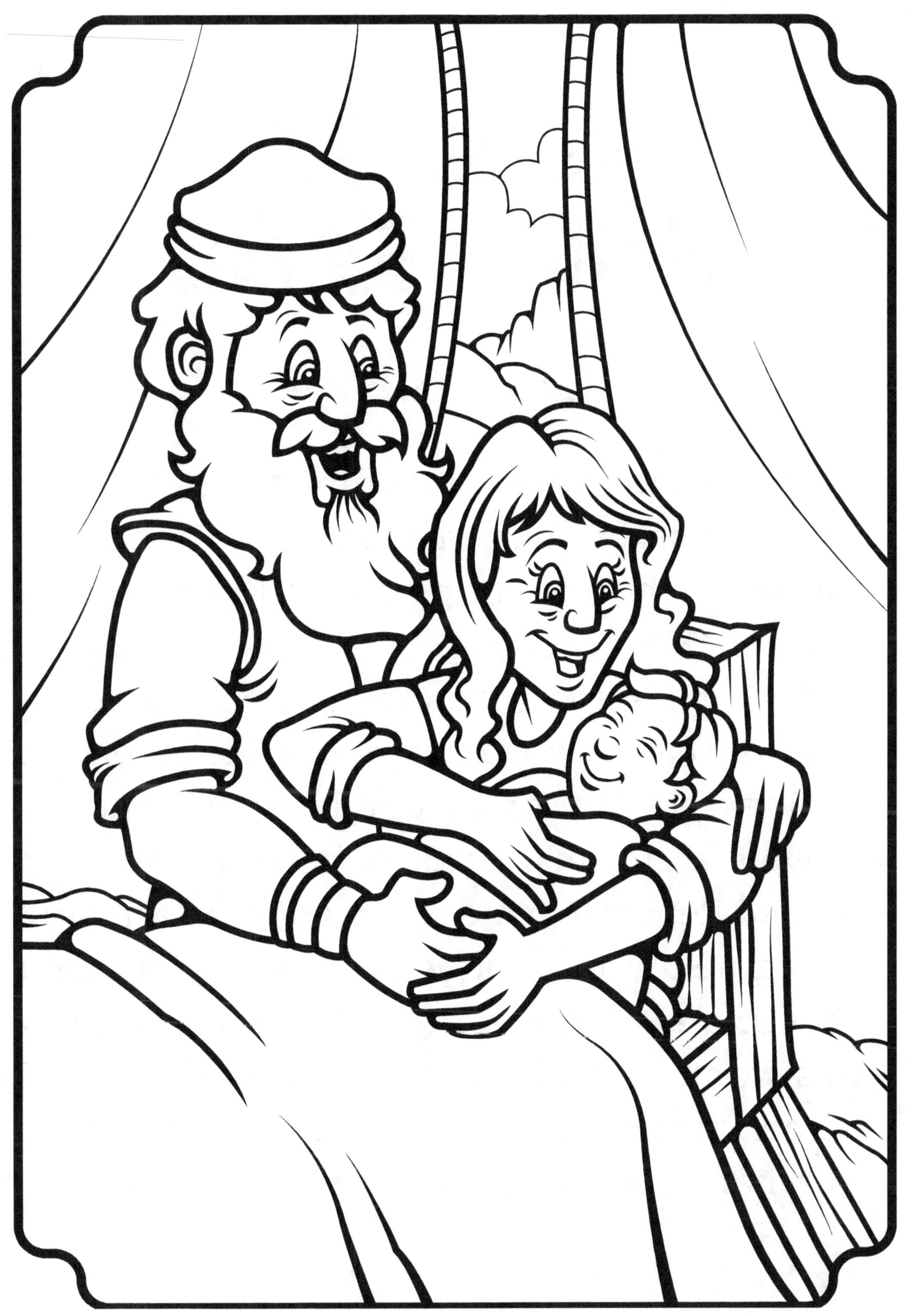

A WIFE FOR ISAAC

GENESIS 24

Isaac grew up! Soon it was time to get married. Abraham asked one of his servants to find a wife for Isaac. The servant promised to do his best to do so. He loaded up some camels with gifts and supplies and rode off into the dry desert to find Isaac a woman to marry. He prayed to God to help him find a good woman, and his prayers were answered! A beautiful woman named Rebekah came up and offered him and his camels a drink of water. She worked hard watering all of the camels. The servant knew this woman was kind and thought she would be perfect for Isaac. He took Rebekah back to Abraham, and she and Isaac were married.

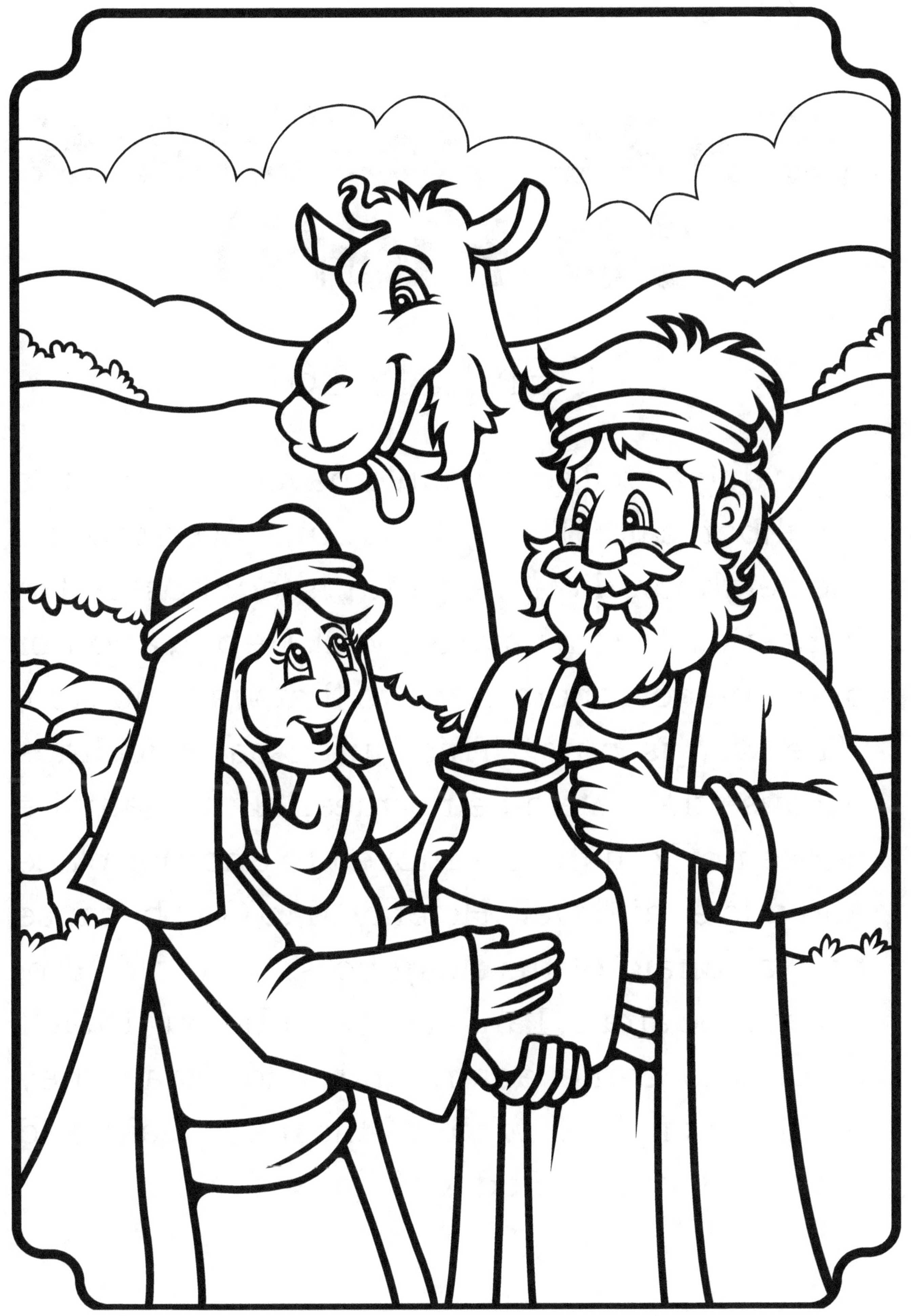

ISAAC REFUSES TO FIGHT

GENESIS 26

Isaac dug a well so he could have water. Isaac's neighbors said, "The water is ours!" Even though the neighbors didn't help him, Isaac chose not to fight and let them have the well. He dug another one. The neighbors came to that well and said, "The well is ours!" This hurt Isaac's feelings because they were being mean. But again, he chose not to fight. He moved to another place and dug a third well. He prayed to God because he was afraid of his neighbors. God told him, "Do not be afraid, I am always with you." Isaac's neighbors came again and told Isaac they would not fight anymore. This made Isaac and his family happy. God took care of Isaac.

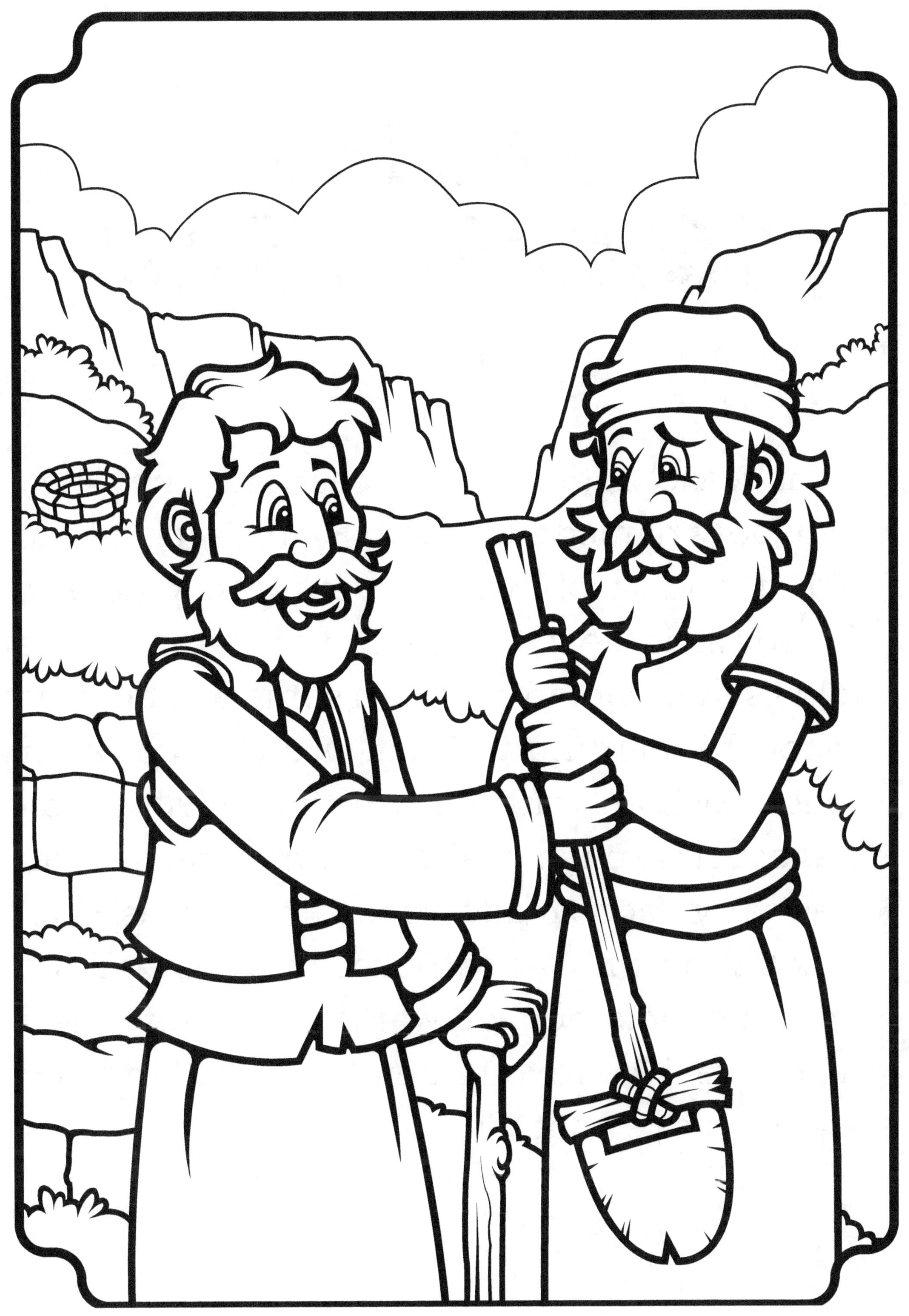

JACOB TRICKS ESAU

GENESIS 27

After Isaac and Rebekah married, they had twin boys named Jacob and Esau. Esau was the oldest, and Jacob was the youngest. One day, Jacob made stew and instead of sharing it, he told Esau he would give him some if Esau gave Jacob his birthright. That wasn't nice! After Jacob got Esau's birthright, he tricked his daddy Isaac too! He put hair all over him because Esau was hairy. Jacob made Isaac think he was Esau! Jacob should not have tricked his brother Esau, or his father Isaac. God wants us to treat others with love. We are to remember to be kind and loving to one another.

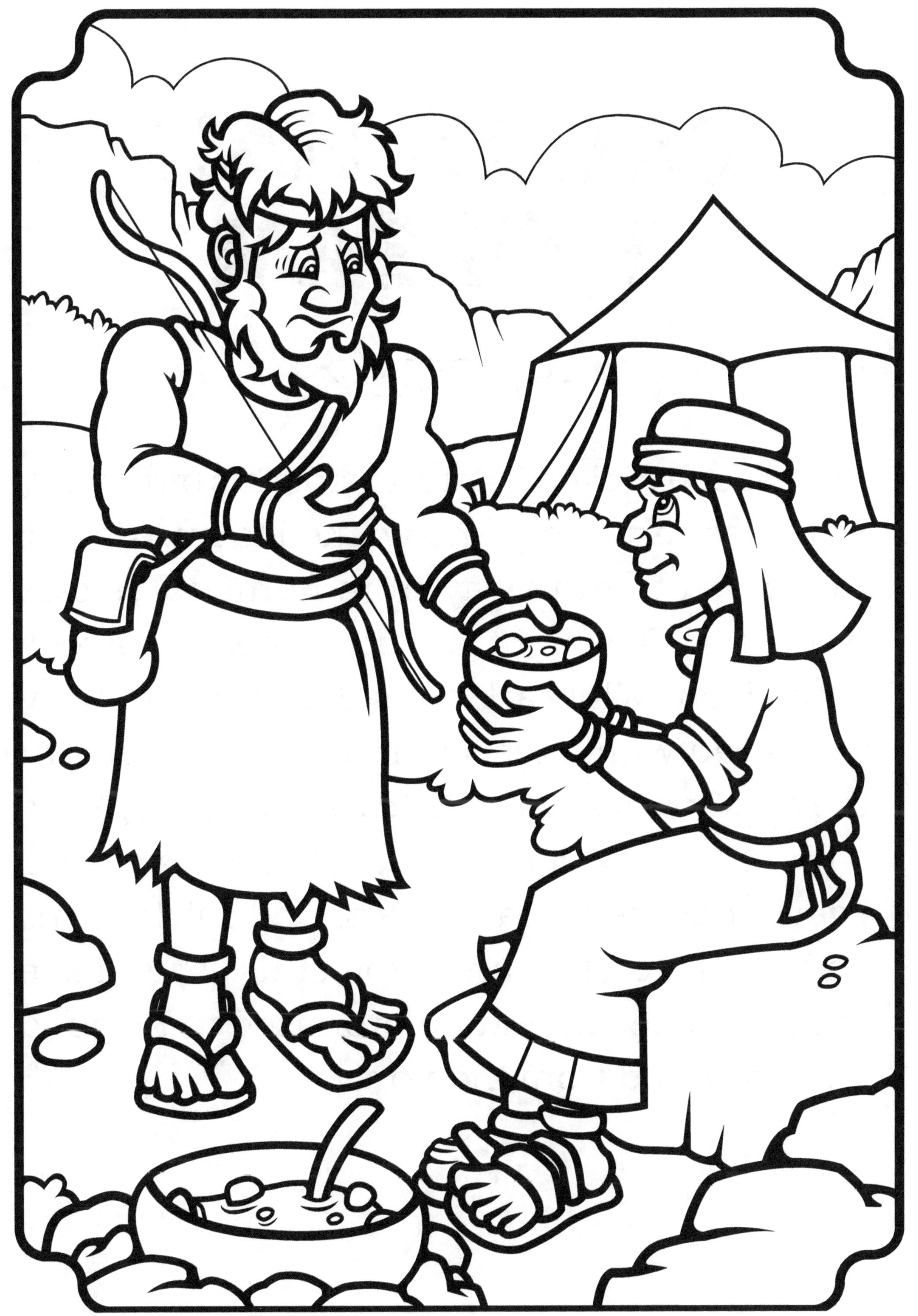

JACOB HAS A DREAM

GENESIS 28

After Jacob tricked Esau and stole his birthright, Esau was very angry and wanted to hurt Jacob. Jacob had to run away from home to be safe from Esau. One night, he laid his head on a rock for a pillow. While asleep, Jacob saw a stairway to heaven with angels going up and down. At the top, God was there! God said to Jacob, "I am with you and will keep you wherever you go." Even when we do bad things, God still loves us and wants to bless and protect us. This made Jacob feel better, and he promised to be good and obey God from then on.

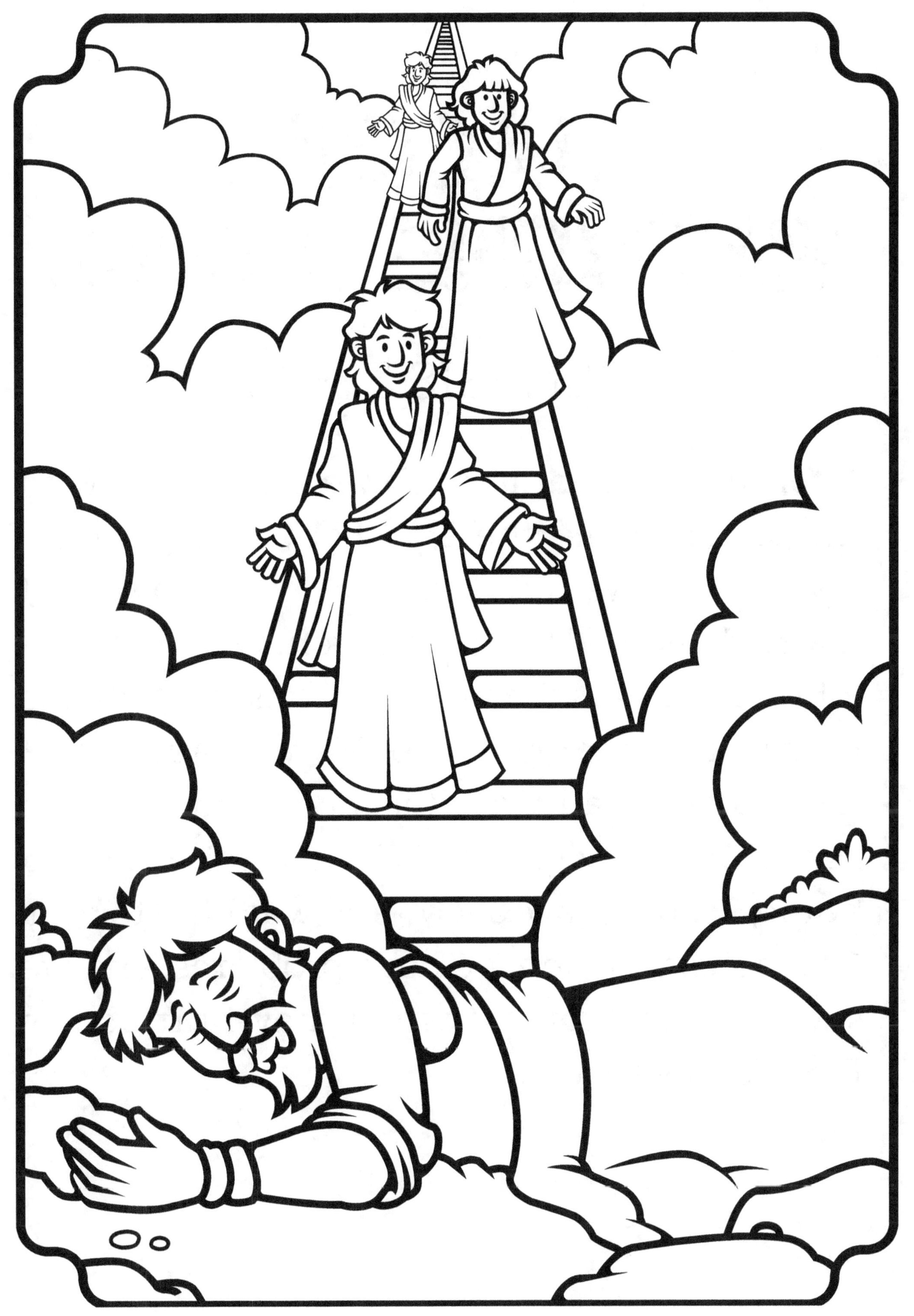

JACOB RETURNS HOME

GENESIS 32-33

After Jacob's dream, Jacob went on to live with his uncle. While there, he got many sheep, goats, donkeys, and camels. Jacob also got married and had many children. One day, God told Jacob it was time to go back home with his family. This scared Jacob. He was afraid that his brother Esau was still mad at him. Jacob asked God to help him. When Jacob returned home, Esau forgave Jacob and was kind to him! God helps us when we have problems, and we should forgive others when they hurt us like Esau forgave Jacob.

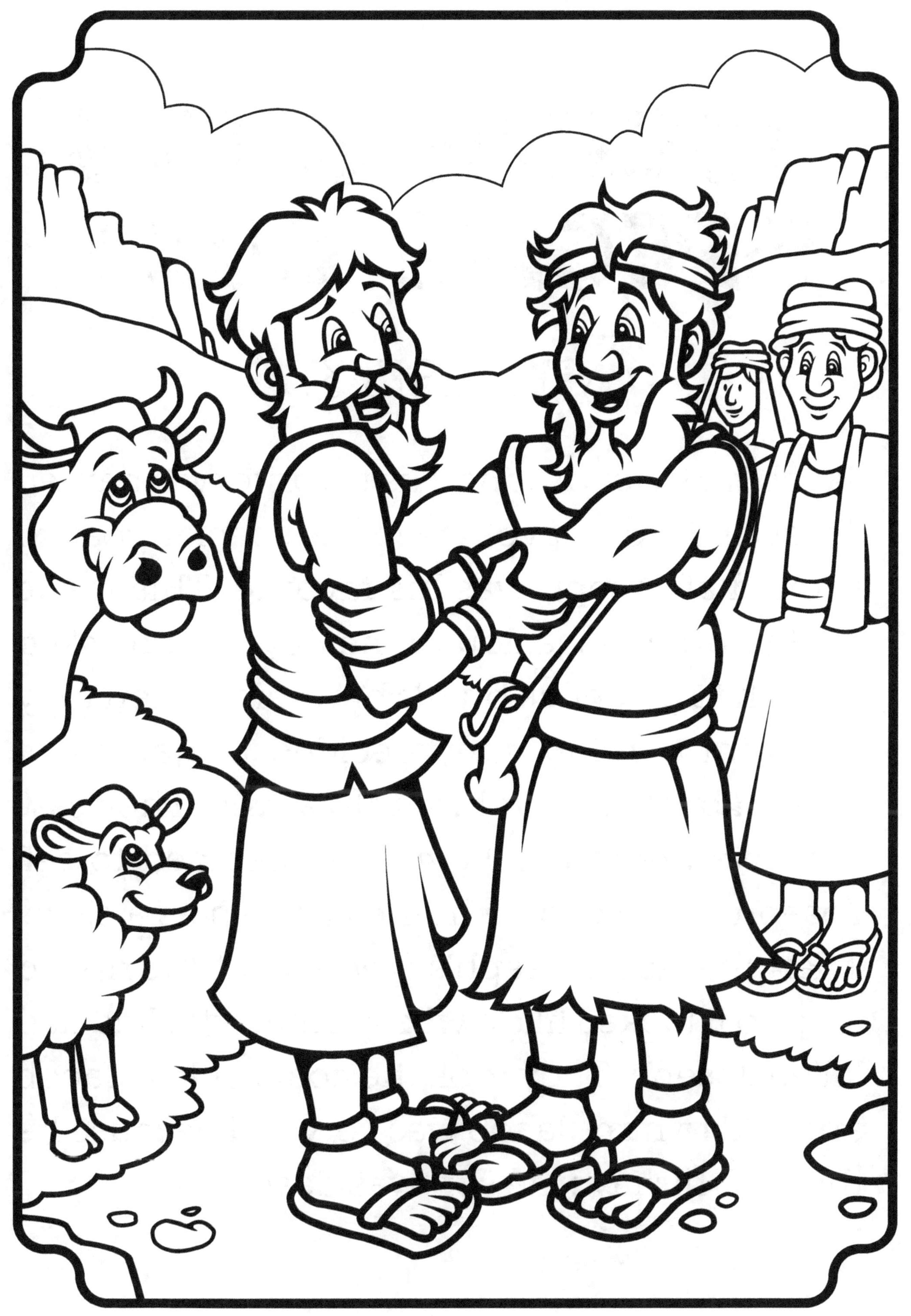

JOSEPH & HIS SPECIAL COAT

GENESIS 37

Jacob had a lot of sons. His favorite was named Joseph. Jacob gave Joseph a special coat to show that Joseph was his favorite. This made his big brothers jealous. One day, Jacob asked Joseph to go check on his brothers. When they saw him coming, they decided to get rid of Joseph by throwing him into a well. They saw a caravan going to Egypt and decided to sell Joseph to the people in the caravan as a slave. Then, they took Joseph's special coat and ripped it up so it looked like a wild animal attacked had killed Joseph. They took the coat back to Jacob and lied to him. Jacob was very sad because he thought his favorite son was dead.

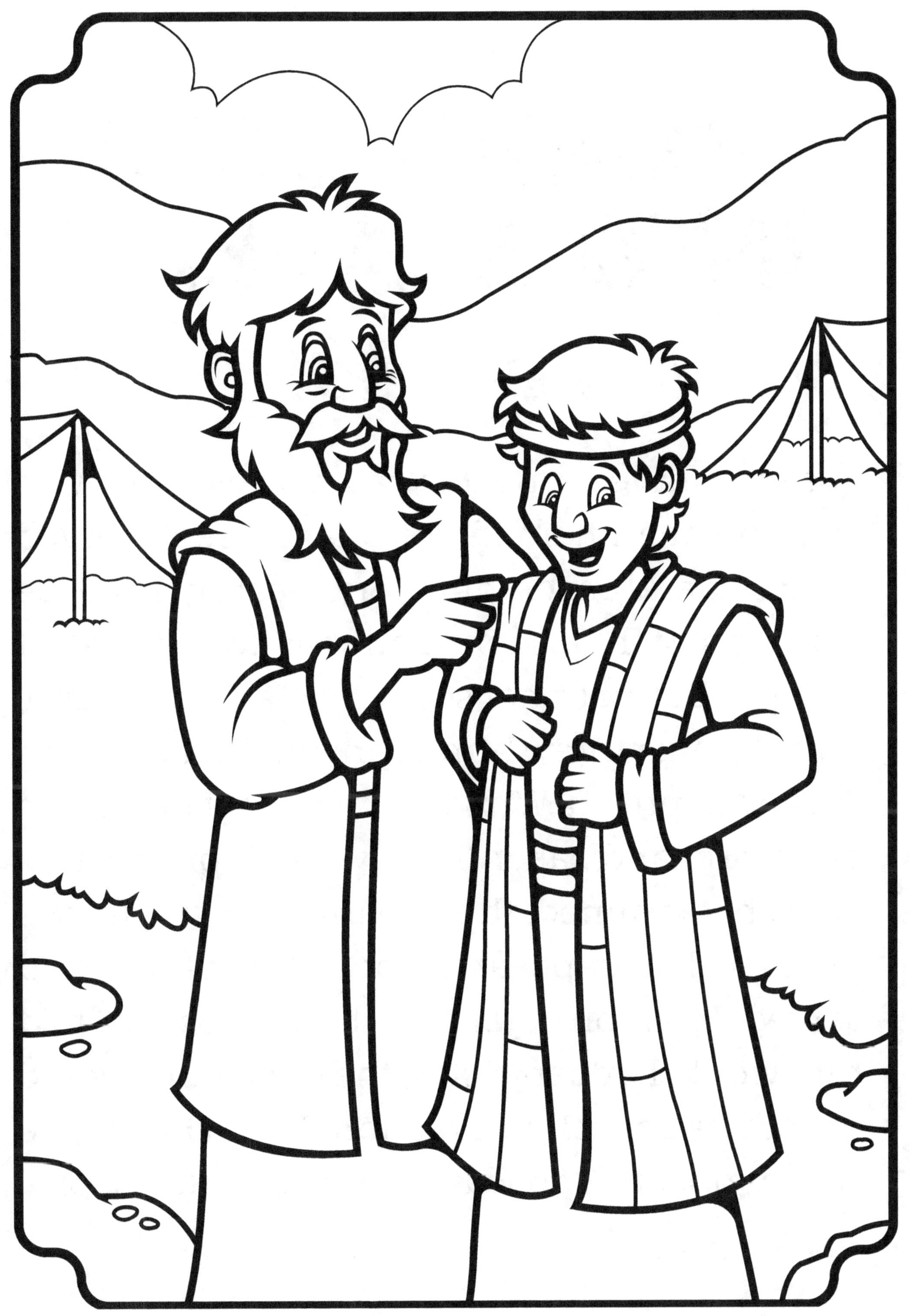

JOSEPH SOLD INTO SLAVERY

GENESIS 39

Joseph arrived in Egypt as a slave and was sold to a man named Potiphar. Joseph served Potiphar and made him very wealthy because God was with Joseph. Potiphar was proud of Joseph. But Potiphar's wife lied about Joseph, and Potiphar threw him in prison. God was with Joseph in prison. While there, he met Pharaoh's cupbearer and baker. They were in prison, too. Joseph explained the meaning of their two dreams. The cupbearer got out of prison and served Pharaoh again, just like Joseph told him would happen! Soon, the cupbearer would introduce Joseph to Pharaoh. Even though he was in prison, God was taking care of Joseph.

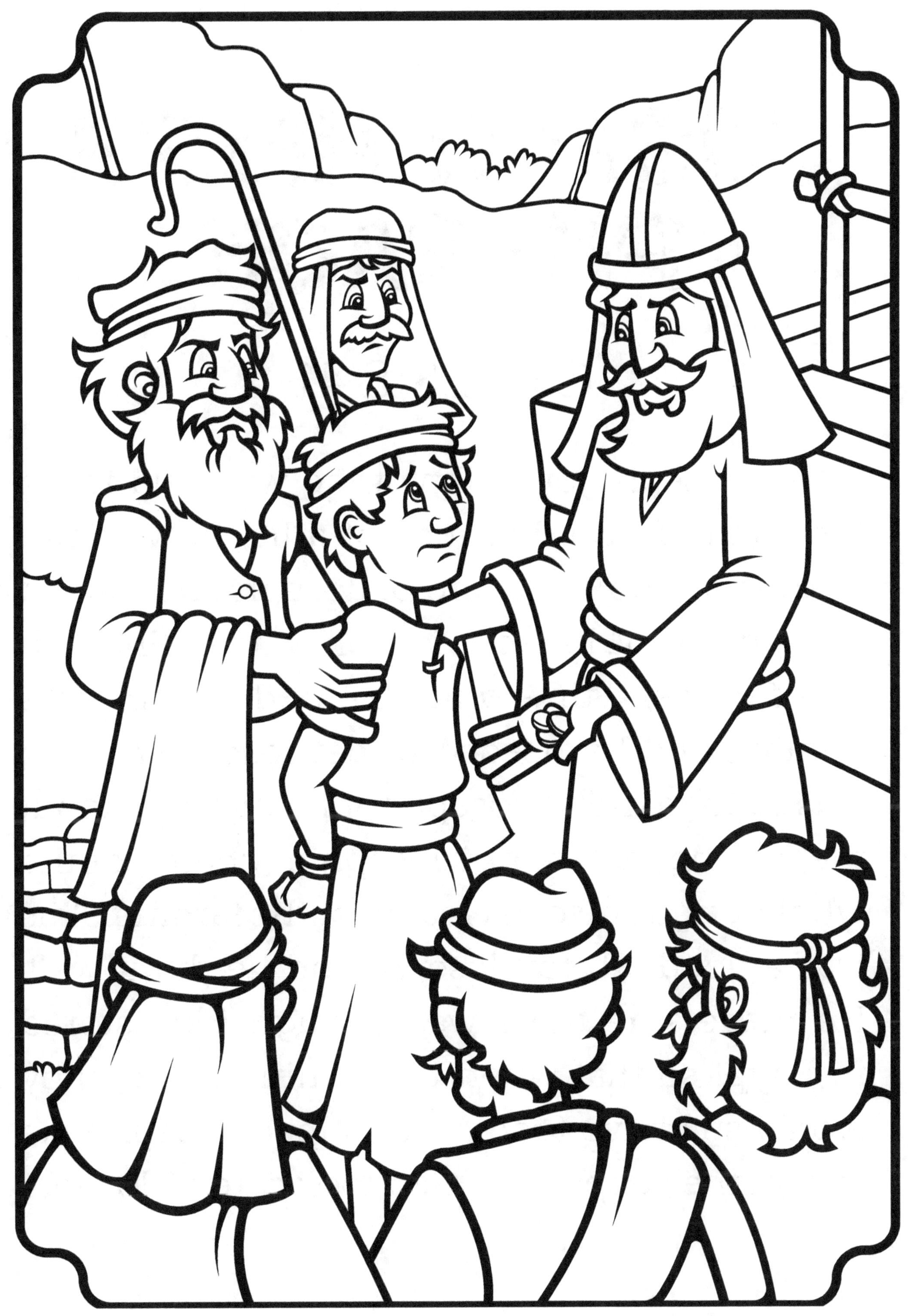

JOSEPH HELPS PHARAOH

GENESIS 41

When Joseph got to Egypt, he was sold to an Egyptian official. Because of a lie, he was put in prison. God took care of Joseph and helped Joseph talk to Pharaoh! Joseph warned Pharaoh of a famine, a time with no food or rain, was coming and he needed to get ready. Pharaoh was so thankful to Joseph for telling him about the famine that he put Joseph in charge of the whole kingdom to get ready for the famine! This was a good job for Joseph, and he did it well. He made sure there was enough food stored in Egypt so that when the famine came, they would still have food. God helped Joseph take care of the people, and God took care of Joseph.

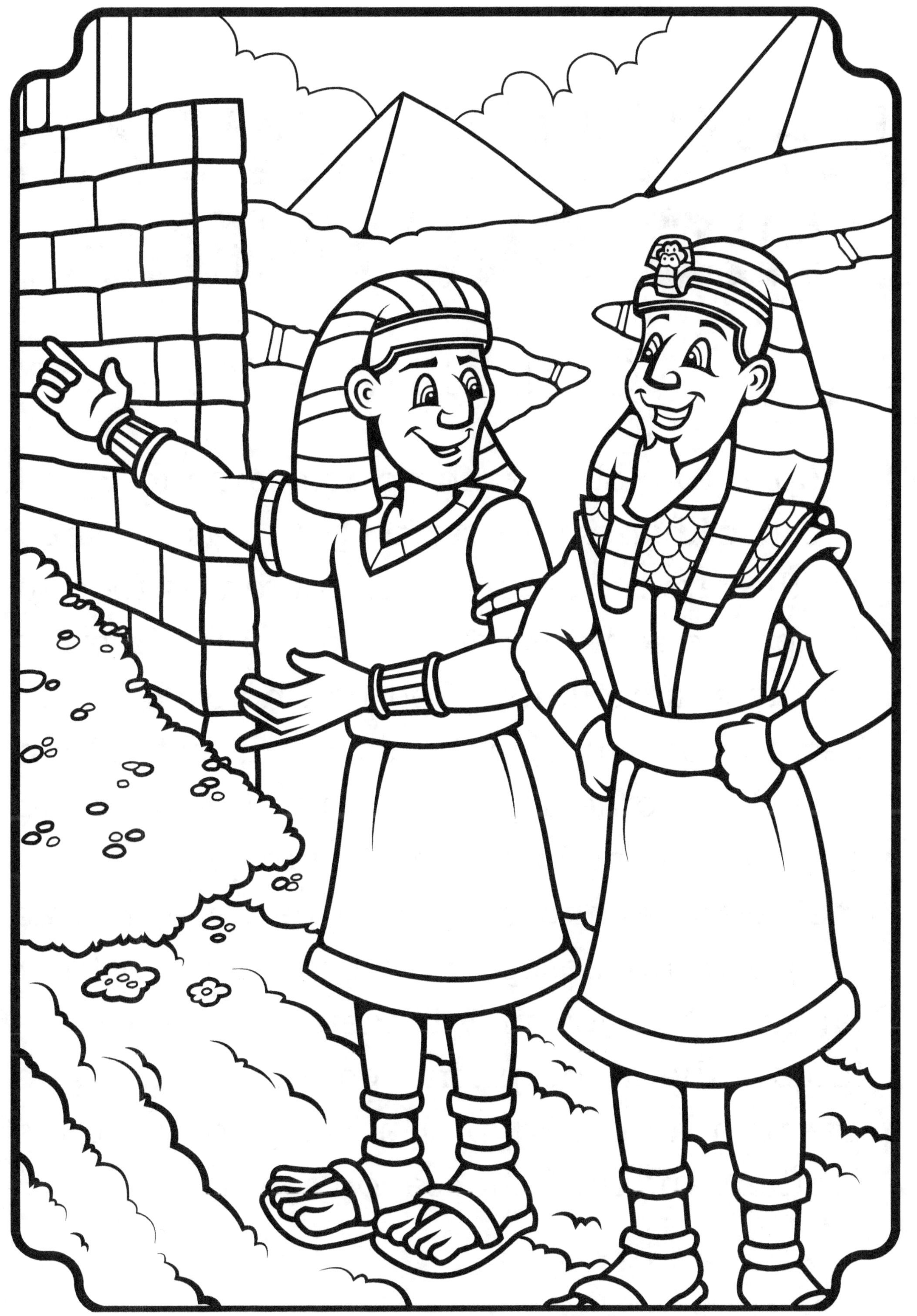

JOSEPH FORGIVES HIS BROTHERS

GENESIS 42-47

People from all over the place came to Egypt because, thanks to Joseph, Egypt was prepared for the famine. Jacob heard there was food in Egypt and sent his sons to get some. Joseph's brothers didn't know God had helped Joseph become an important ruler in Egypt. When Joseph's brothers got to Egypt, they asked to buy food from Joseph and didn't even know they were talking to Joseph because he was all grown up! Joseph asked them about their family. When Joseph told them who he was, he forgave them! Joseph invited them all to come live near him in Egypt. He was glad to see his brothers and his father Jacob again.

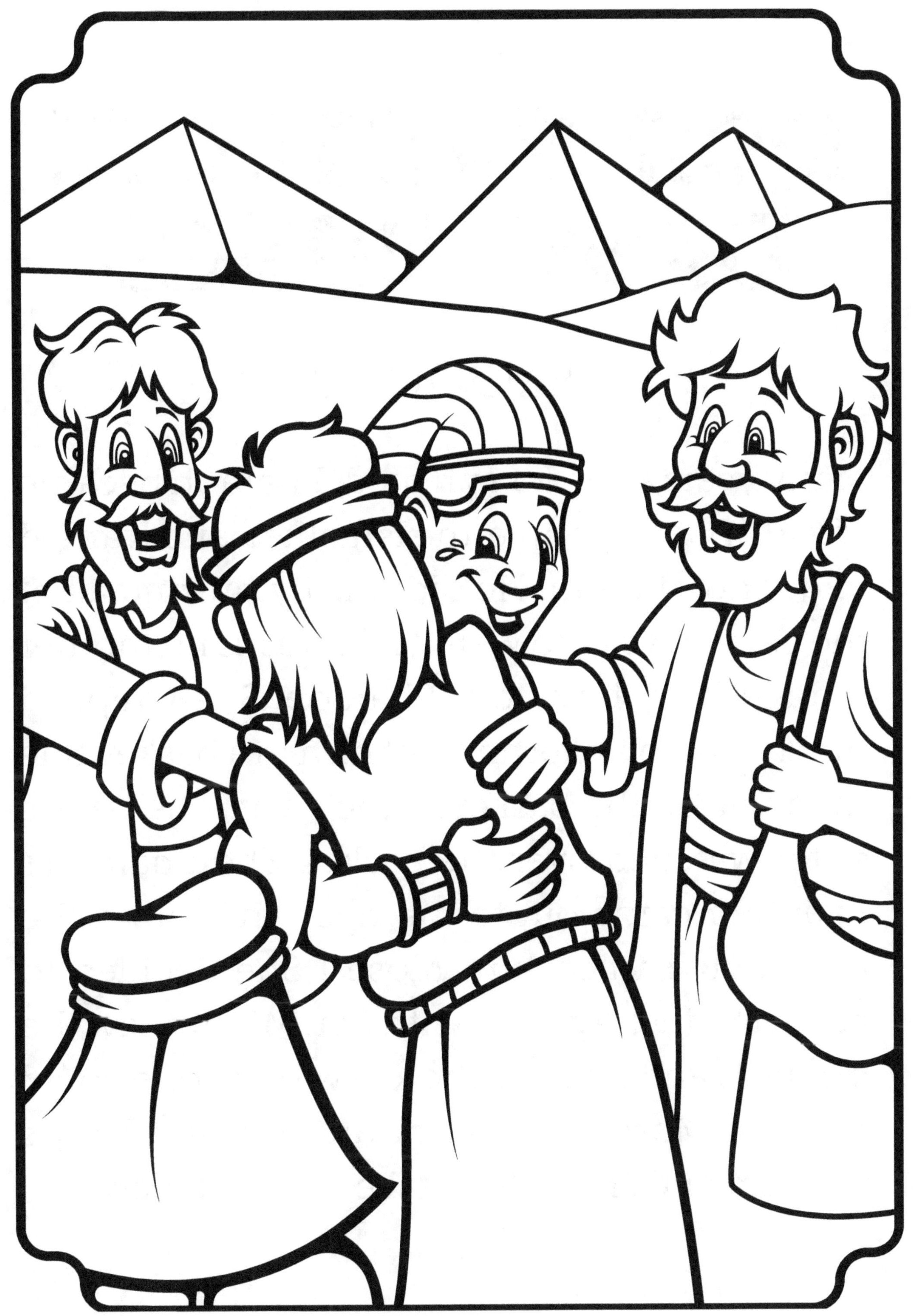

GOD PROTECTS BABY MOSES

EXODUS 2

Many years after Joseph died, Pharaoh became afraid of God's people, the Israelites, and wanted to get rid of them. He did this by hurting all of the baby boys who were Israelites. One mother hid her baby boy from Pharaoh. She wrapped him up in a blanket and put him in a basket. She then placed the basket in the river. The baby's sister watched over the basket. The Pharaoh's daughter came out to the river and found the baby and named him Moses! She decided to keep him in the palace with her. Miriam saw the princess and told her she knew someone could care for Moses. She went and got the baby's mother, and she helped take care of Moses.

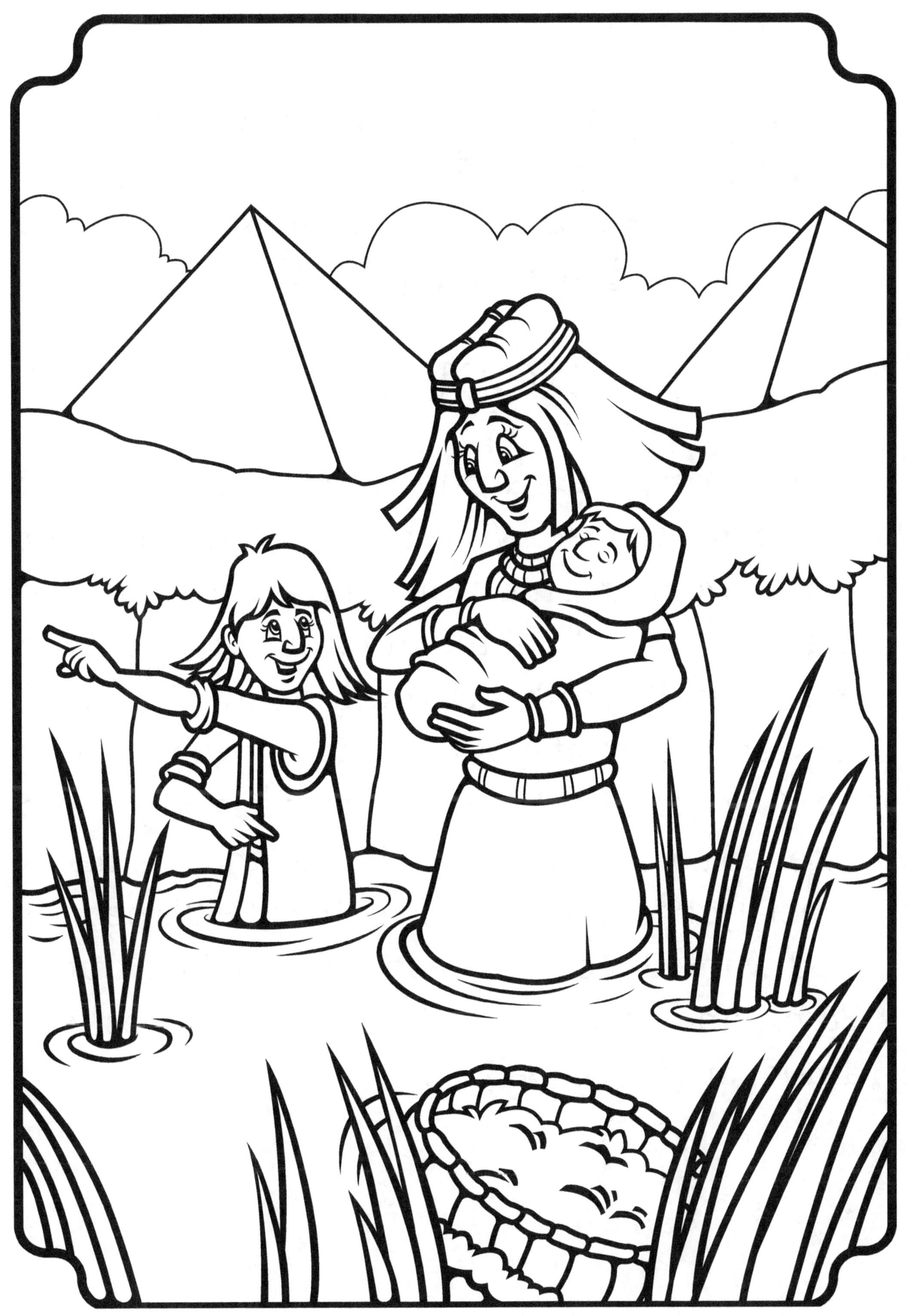

MOSES TALKS TO GOD

EXODUS 3-4

When Moses grew up, he lived in the desert and took care of sheep. While he was with the sheep, Moses went up on a mountain and saw a bush that was on fire! But the fire wasn't burning up the bush! From the burning bush, God said, "Moses! Take off your shoes because you're on holy ground." Moses took off his shoes and listened to God. God told Moses that he had a special job for Moses to do to help God's people. God wanted Moses to lead the Israelites out of Egypt and to the Promised Land. Moses was afraid, but he obeyed God.

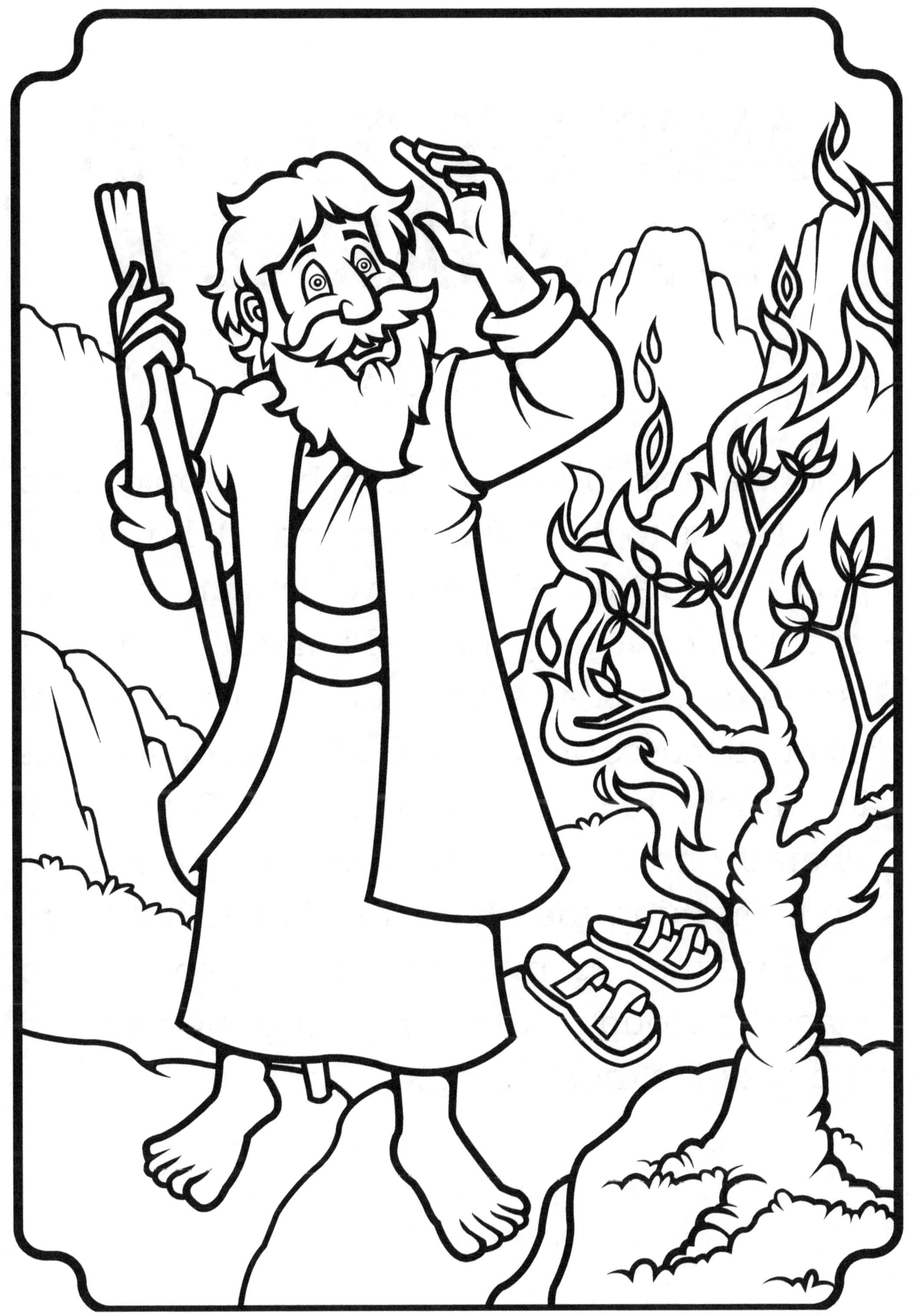

MOSES TALKS TO PHARAOH

EXODUS 7-12

God wanted Moses to help his people. God told Moses to go to Pharaoh and tell him to let God's people go. Pharaoh was mean to God's people. For a long time, Pharaoh made the Israelites work as slaves. Pharaoh would not listen to Moses or God, so God sent Ten Plagues to punish Pharaoh and the land of Egypt until Pharaoh finally gave in. God's people packed up everything they had, and Moses led them out into the desert. To guide the people, God placed a cloud in the sky during the day and fire to guide them at night.

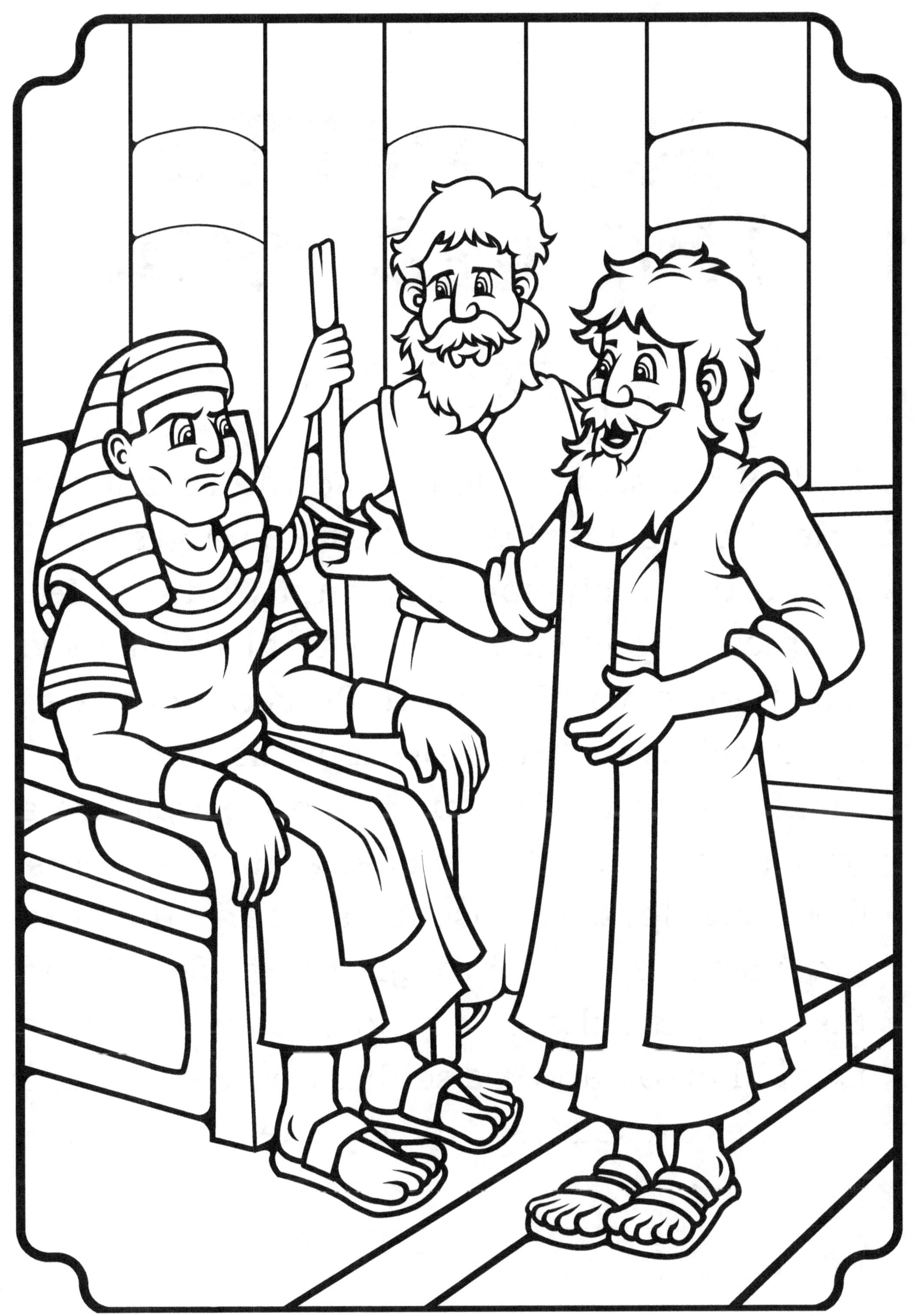

GOD PARTS THE RED SEA

EXODUS 14

God told Moses to go to Pharaoh and order him to let the Israelites leave Egypt. Pharaoh said he would, but he changed his mind. God sent Ten Plagues to punish Pharaoh until he allowed Israel to leave. But then Pharaoh changed his mind again. Pharaoh sent his soldiers to make the Israelites return. God's people were trapped between the Red Sea and the soldiers! God told Moses to raise his staff and the Lord provided a dry path through the Red Sea. When they reached the other side, Israel was safe from Pharaoh and his soldiers. Moses and the Israelites trusted God, and God delivered them.

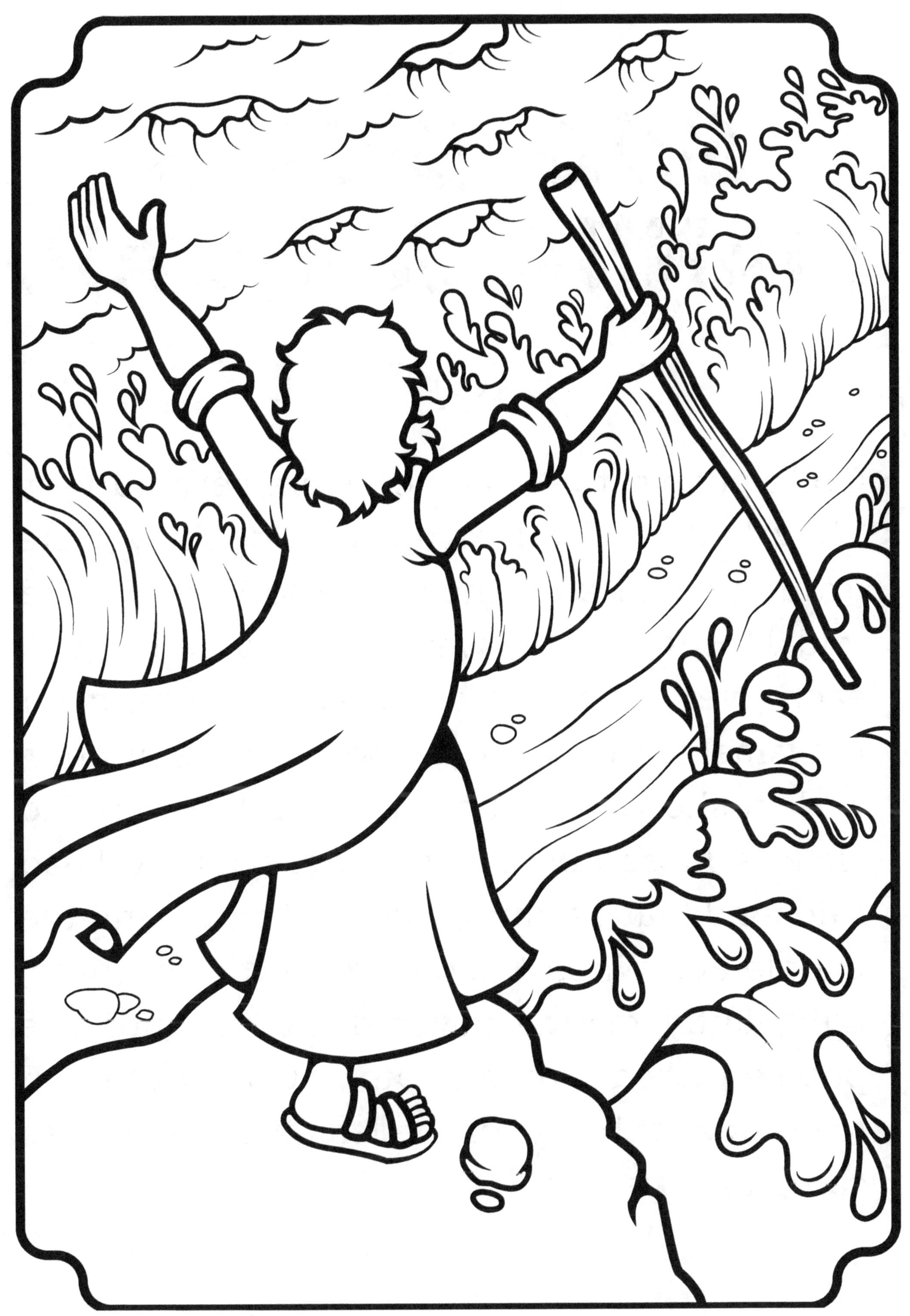

GOD SENDS MANNA & QUAIL

EXODUS 16

God's people, the Israelites, were very hungry. They had no food in the desert. They were grumbling because they were so hungry. God told Moses that he was going to send quail each evening and manna each morning for the Israelites to eat so they wouldn't be hungry, and to show them how powerful and loving He was. Moses told the Israelites what God had said, and that evening, the quail came and the people ate. When they woke in the morning, light, fluffy manna covered the ground. The people picked it up and ate it. God continued to do this each day for the Israelites. God takes care of His people.

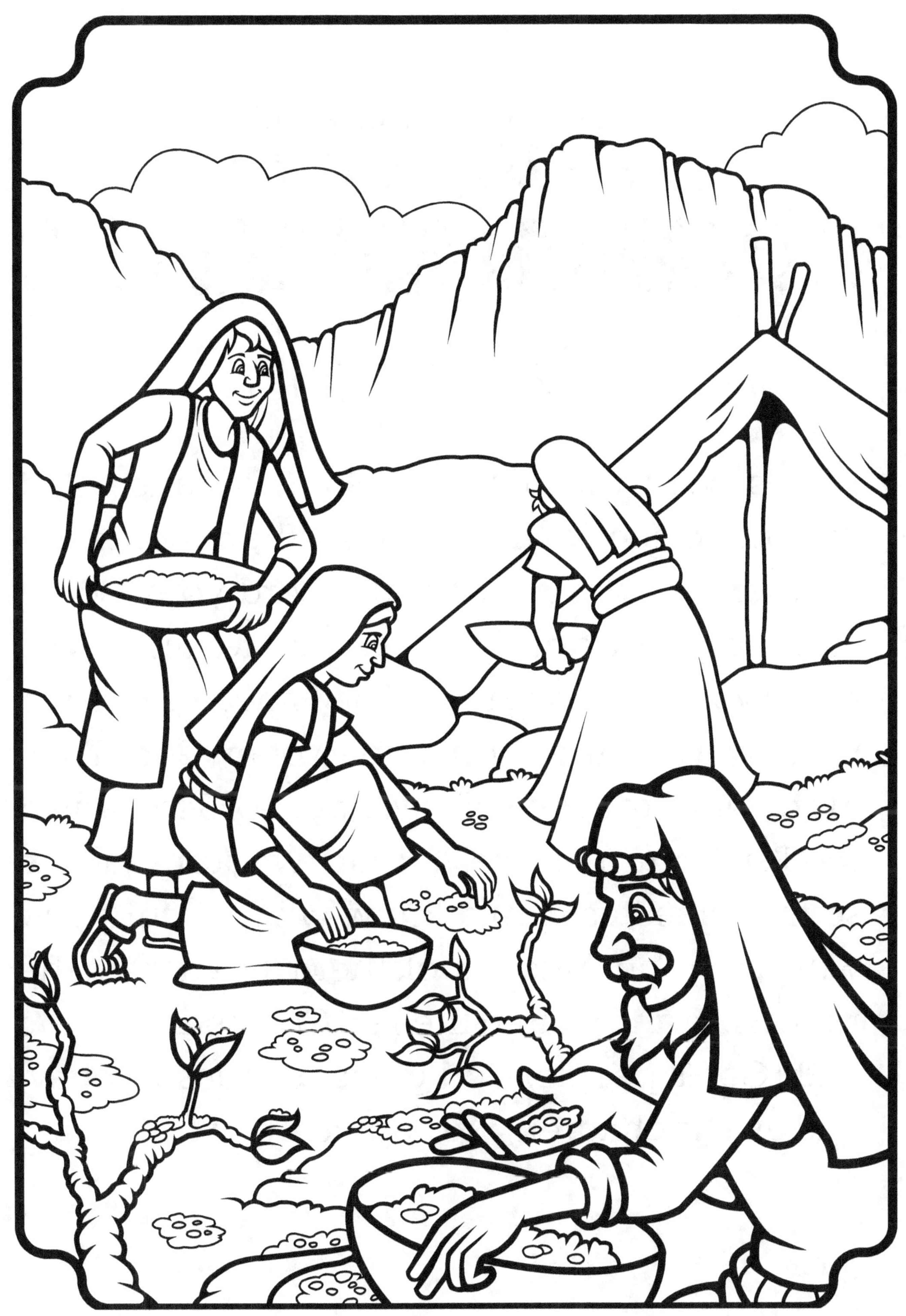

THE TEN COMMANDMENTS

EXODUS 20

Moses went up to Mount Sinai because God wanted to speak with Moses. When Moses got up there, God said, "I am the Lord your God. I rescued you from Egypt. Obey Me, and I will make your nations great." The Israelites needed to know what they could do to obey God. They didn't have the Bible like we do. So God carved the Ten Commandments onto two stone tablets so the Israelites would know what is right and what is wrong. Moses took them down from the mountain and shared the Ten Commandments with God's people. God gives us rules to obey, and as His children, we should obey him.

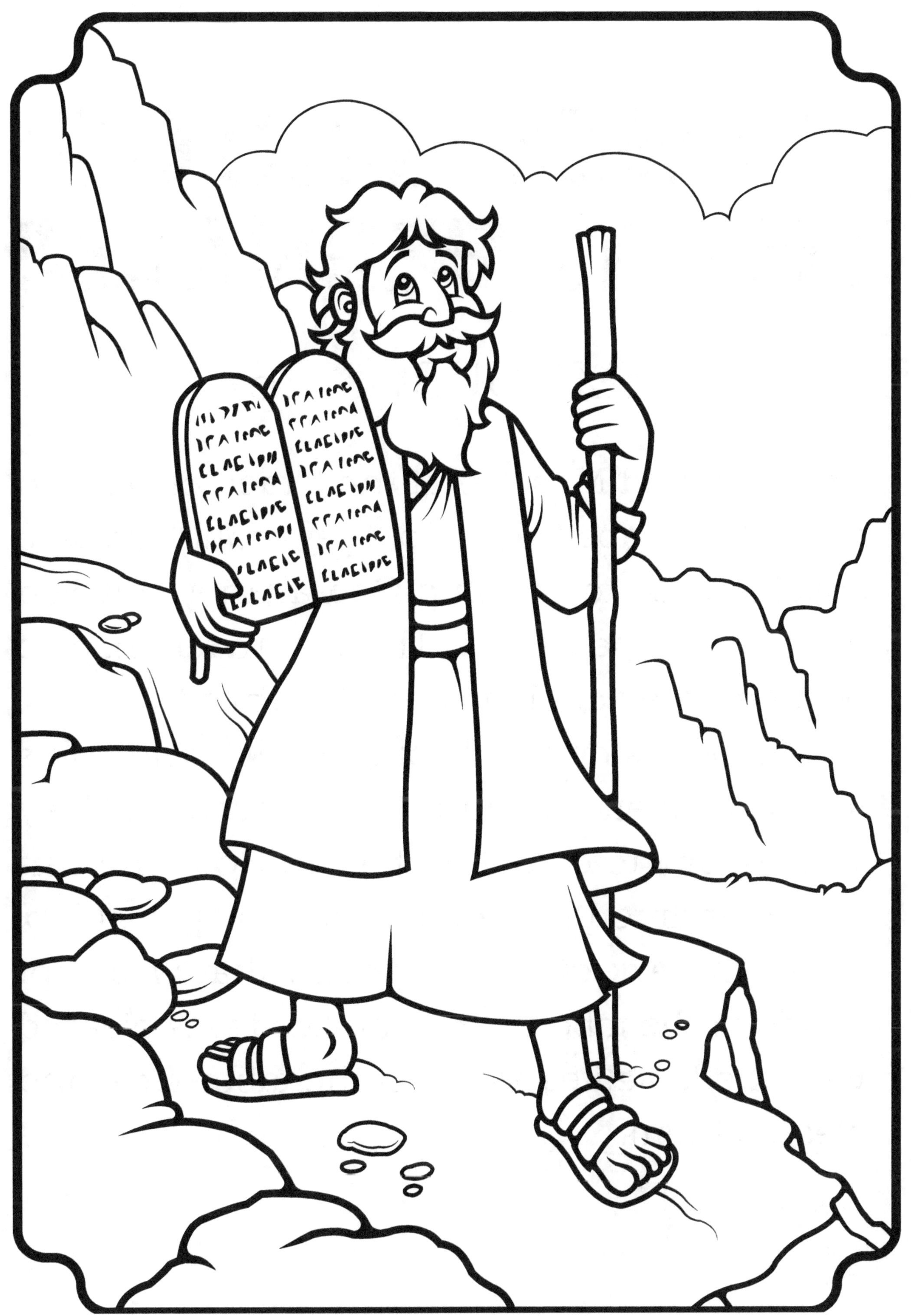

MOSES BUILDS THE TABERNACLE

EXODUS 35-36

The Lord told Moses that the Israelites needed to build a tabernacle so they could have a special place to worship God as they traveled to the Promised Land. The tabernacle had to be a tent they could take apart while traveling. The Israelites brought gold, jewelry, and coins to the workers building the tabernacle. They were happy to give their best to God. The Ten Commandments were placed in a special box called the Ark of the Covenant that was kept inside of the tabernacle. The Lord was pleased with the Israelites work on the tabernacle and blessed them.

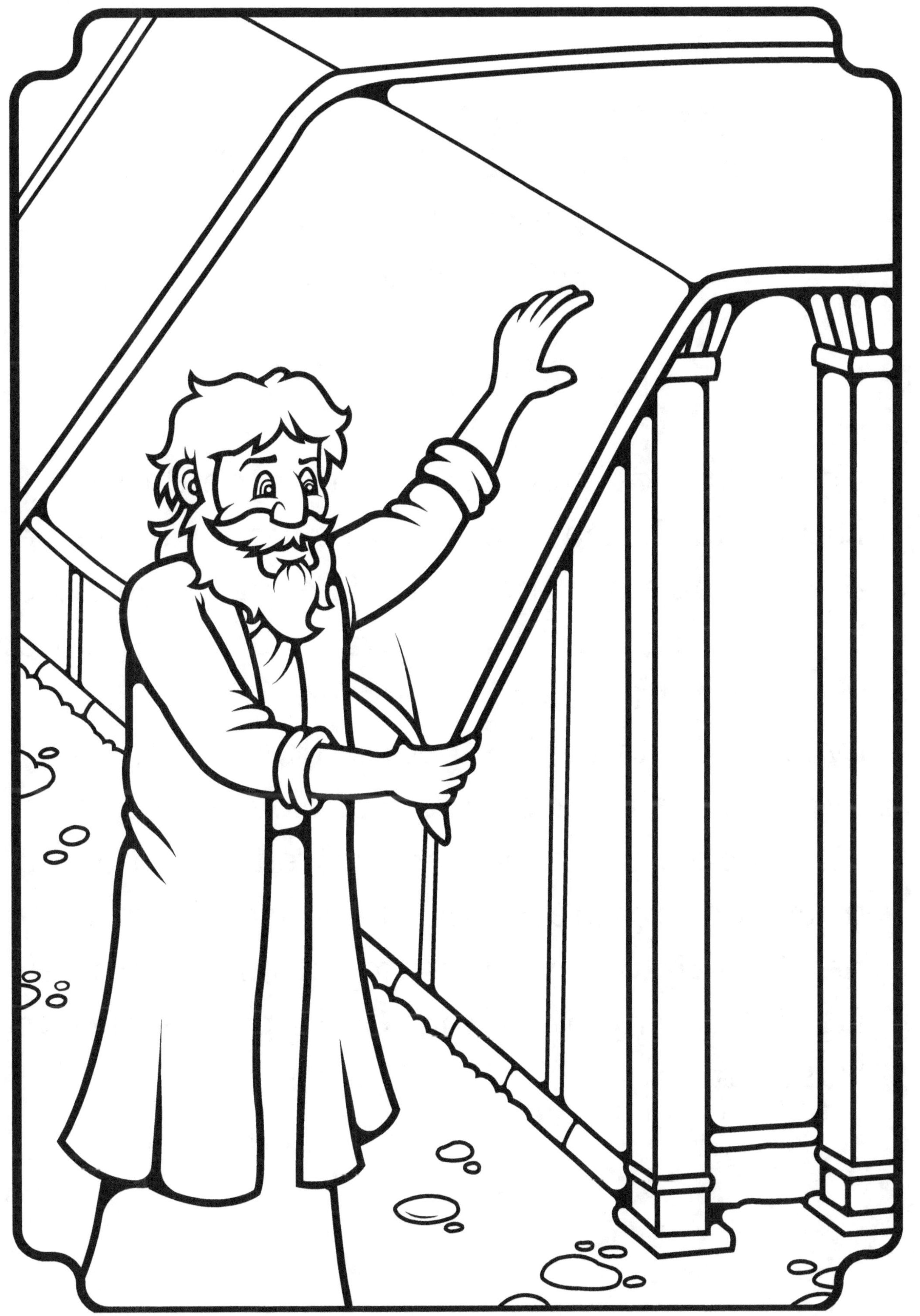

THE TWELVE SPIES

NUMBERS 13-14

The people of Israel arrived near the Promised Land and Canaan, and Moses sent out twelve men to spy out the land. The men returned with big fruit and said it was a beautiful land flowing with milk and with honey, but giants lived in the land. The people there were really big, and their cities were really big and strong! The people of Israel were scared and did not trust God to protect them. Because of this, they had to wait forty years to go into the Promised Land. It is important that God's people always trust him.

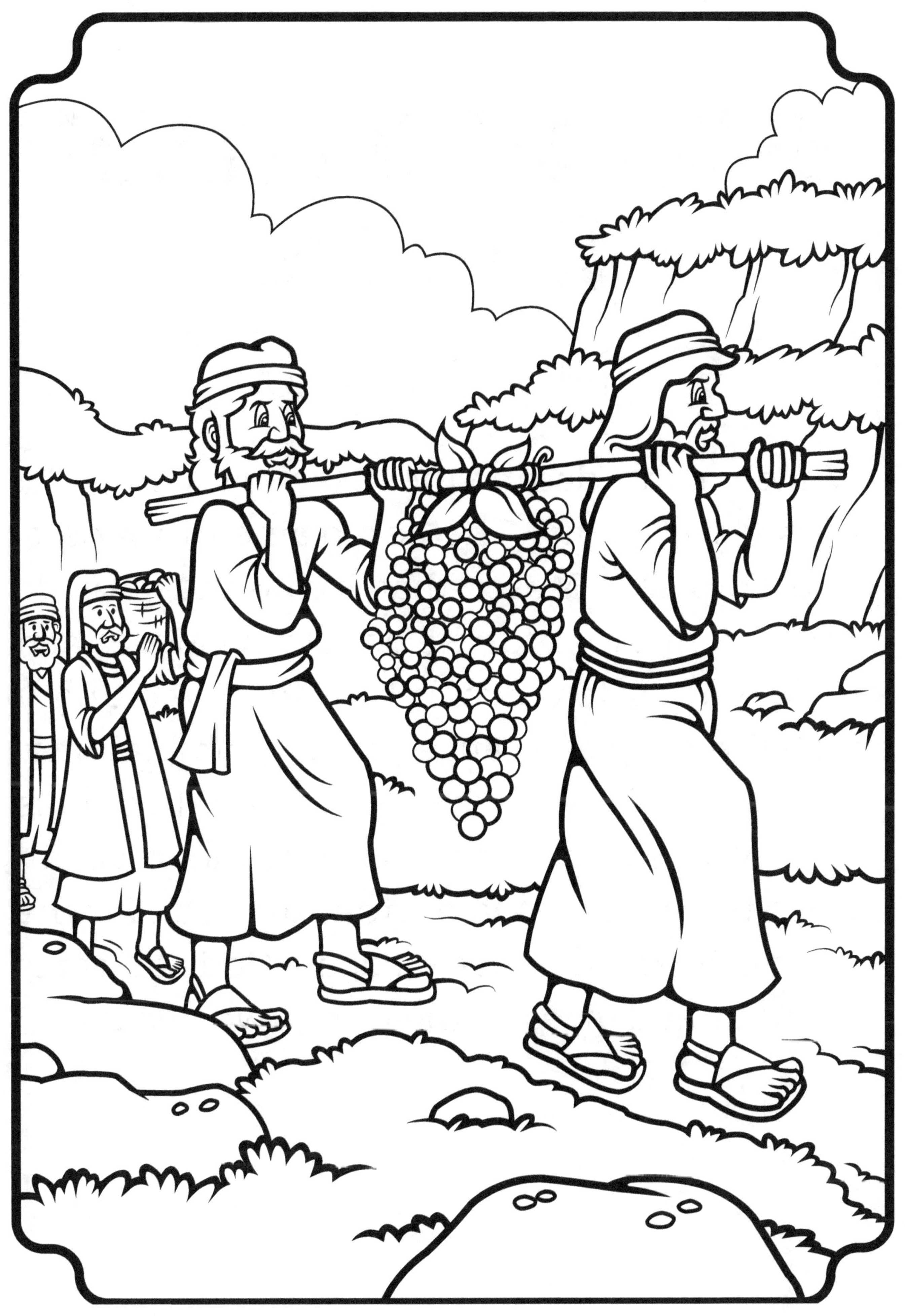

GOD PROVIDES WATER

NUMBERS 20

While in the desert, the Israelites got really thirsty and angry. The complained to Moses. The Lord told Moses that He would provide water from a rock for the people. All Moses had to do was talk to the rock. But Moses was angry with the people because of their complaining. Instead of talking to the rock, he hit it with his staff. Moses disobeyed God's instructions, but God still provided water from the rock for the people. Even when we disobey, God still cares about us and gives us the things we need.

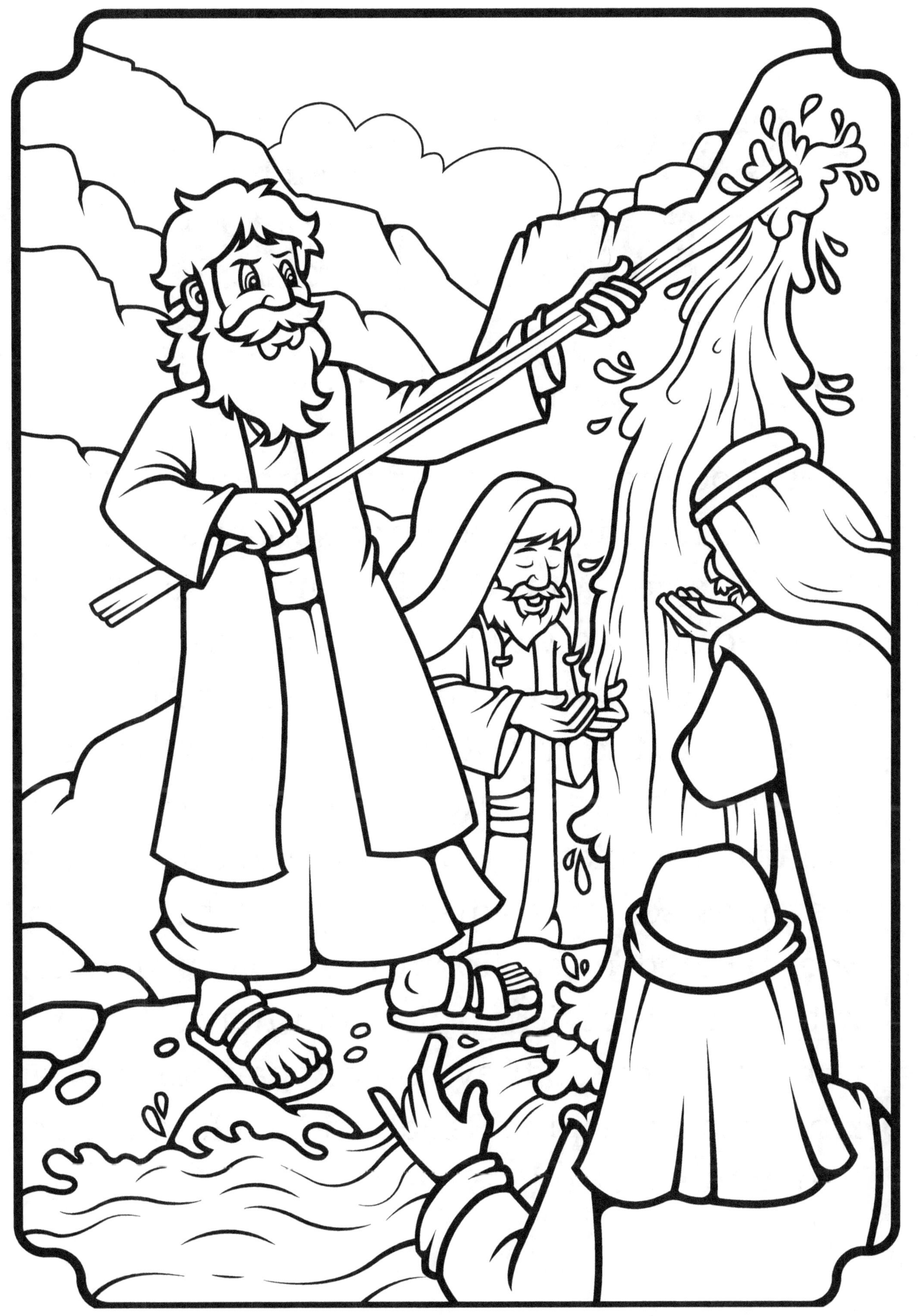

RAHAB HELPS THE SPIES

JOSHUA 2

God appointed a new leader named Joshua to lead the Israelites. God chose Joshua because Joshua spied out the Promised Land and believed that God would help them, even though there were giants and large cities. Joshua sent out spies to the city of Jericho. When the King of Jericho heard about this, he sent soldiers to capture the spies. A woman named Rahab hid the spies so the soldiers couldn't find them. She lowered them down the wall of Jericho with a red rope. The spies told her to leave it in her window so they could repay her for her kindness by keeping Rahab and her family safe. Rahab trusted God.

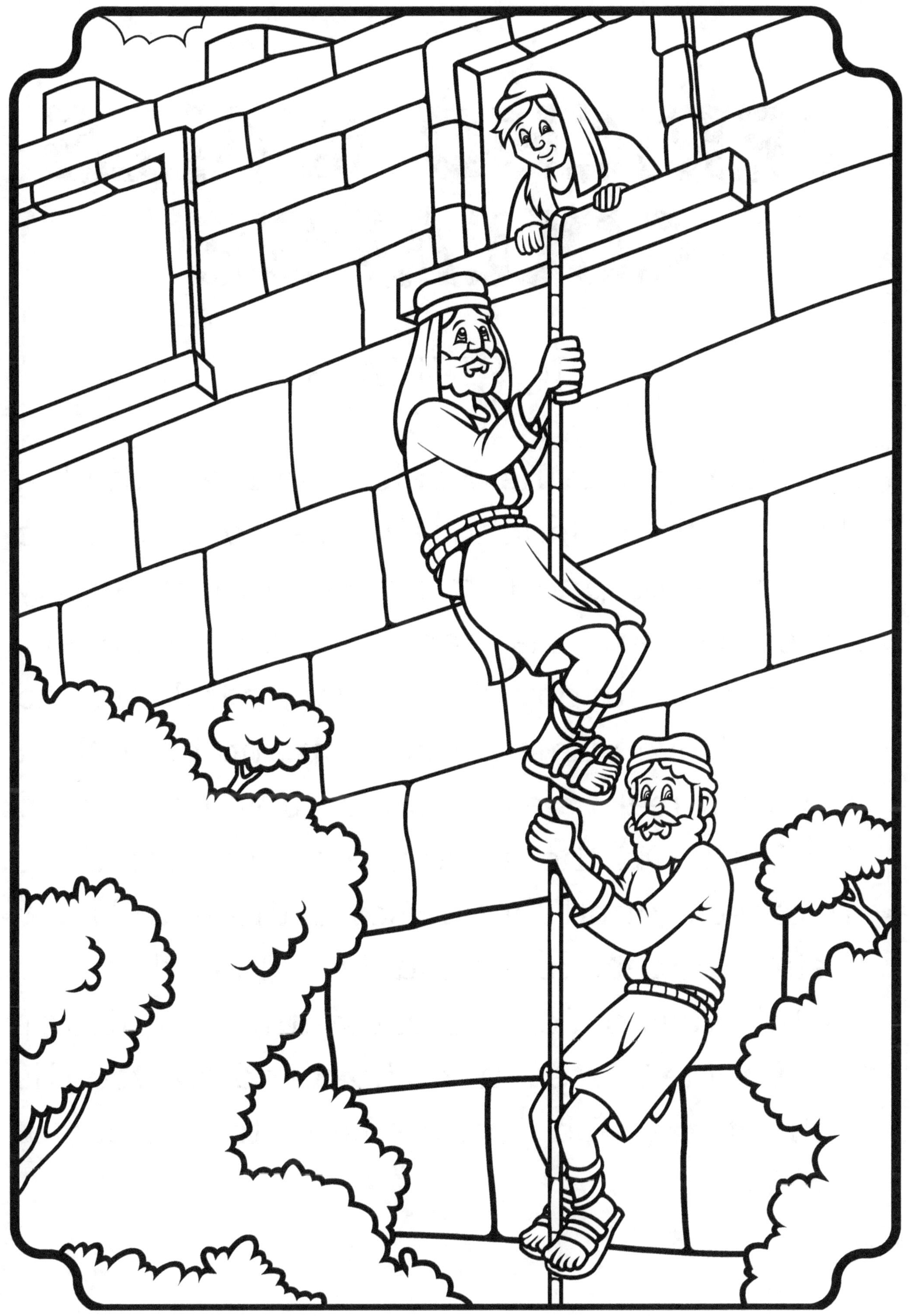

JERICHO WALLS COLLAPSE

JOSHUA 6

God told Joshua he would give Israel the big strong city of Jericho. God asked Joshua to choose seven priests to march around the city once a day for six days and blow their trumpets. On the seventh day, they had to march around the city seven times, then stop and blow their trumpets really, really loudly. Joshua obeyed the Lord. On the seventh day, the Israelites marched around Jericho seven times and blew their trumpets really loudly! When they did so, the walls of Jericho came tumbling down! The people trusted in the Lord and obeyed His instructions. God gave the Israelites the city of Jericho.

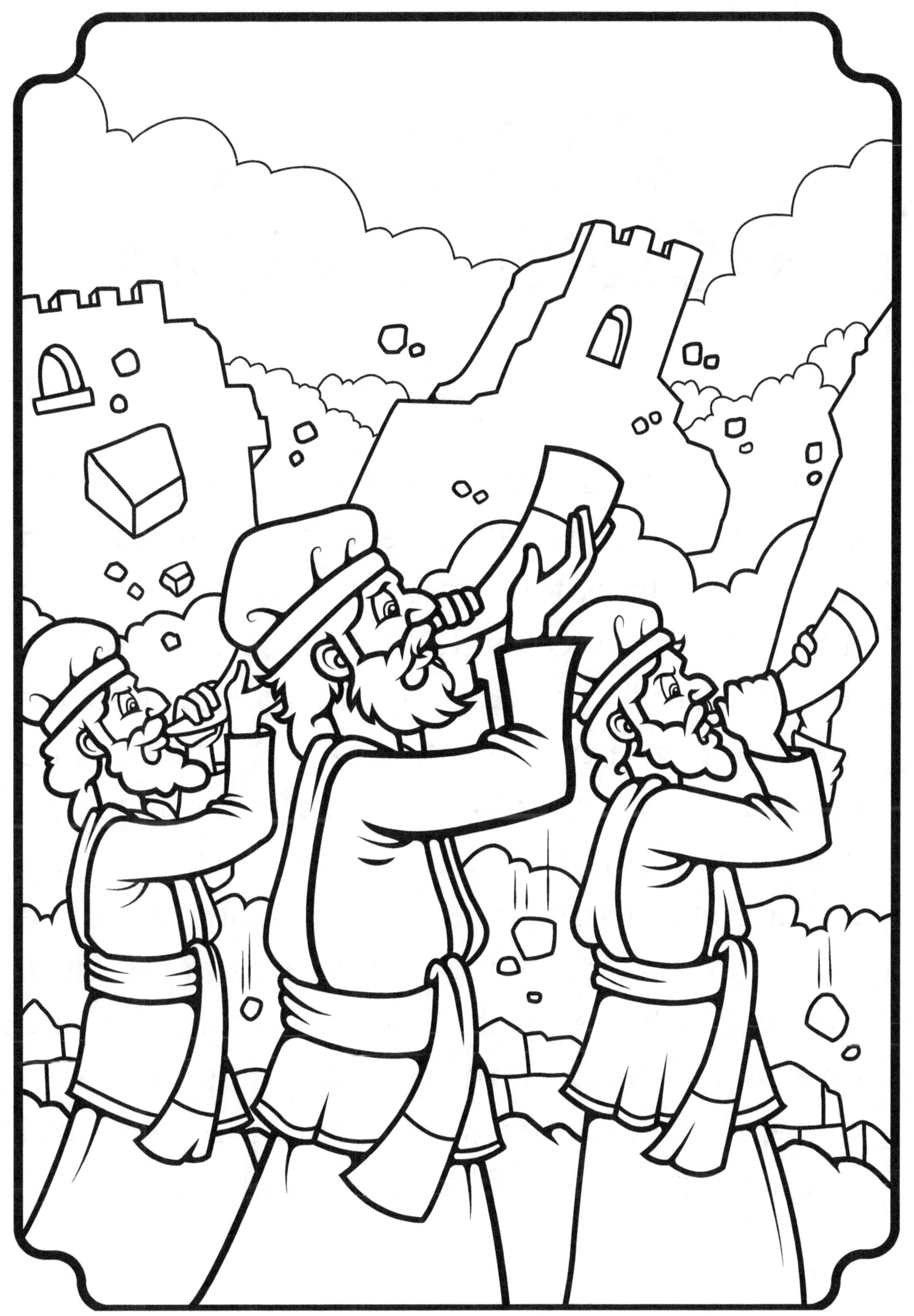

DEBORAH HELPS BARAK

JUDGES 4-5

Deborah was a prophetess for God and had a message for Barak. She told Barak to lead an army into battle, and the Lord would help him win. Barak obeyed, but asked Deborah to go with him. The Israelite army camped on the side of a mountain and saw the Canaanite army racing towards them with their strong horses and fast chariots. But God caused a big thunderstorm that created a lot of mud. The horses and chariots began got stuck in the mud! Deborah told Barak that God was on their side and was helping them. The Israelites were able to defeat the Canaanites because Barack and Deborah obeyed God, and God helped them.

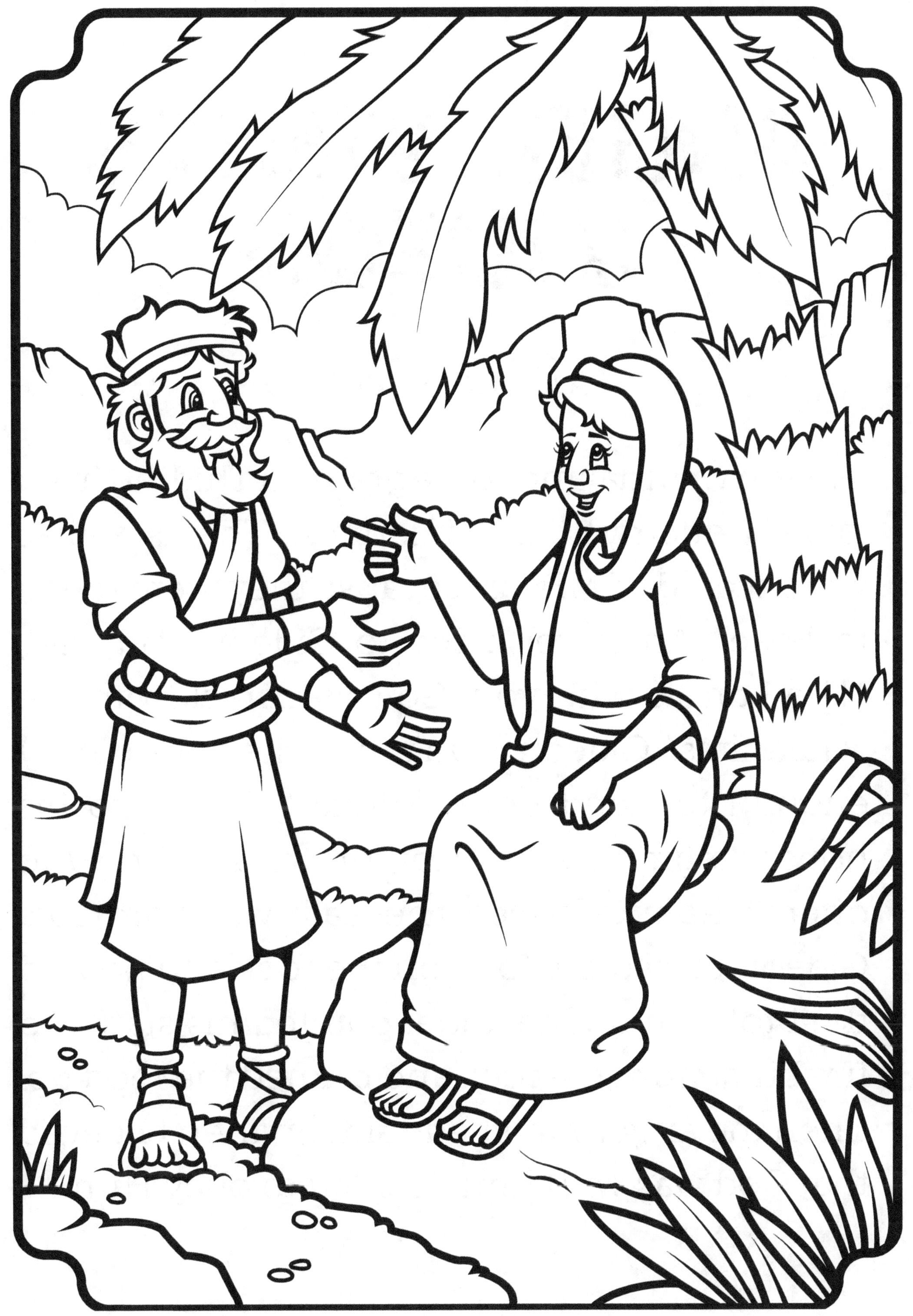

ANGEL VISITS GIDEON

JUDGES 6

Gideon was making some grain and hiding from Israel's enemy, the Midianites. The Israelites were scared of Midian because they were mean to Israel. An angel came to Gideon and said, "The Lord is with you! Go save Israel from the Midianites." Gideon didn't think he was mighty enough to stand up to Midian! He ran to his house to grab some meat, broth, and bread to offer to the angel to see if he really was from God. Gideon placed the food on the rock and poured the broth on it. The angel pointed his staff and fire burst from the rock and burned the food up. Then the angel vanished! Gideon then believed that God was with him decided to obey Him.

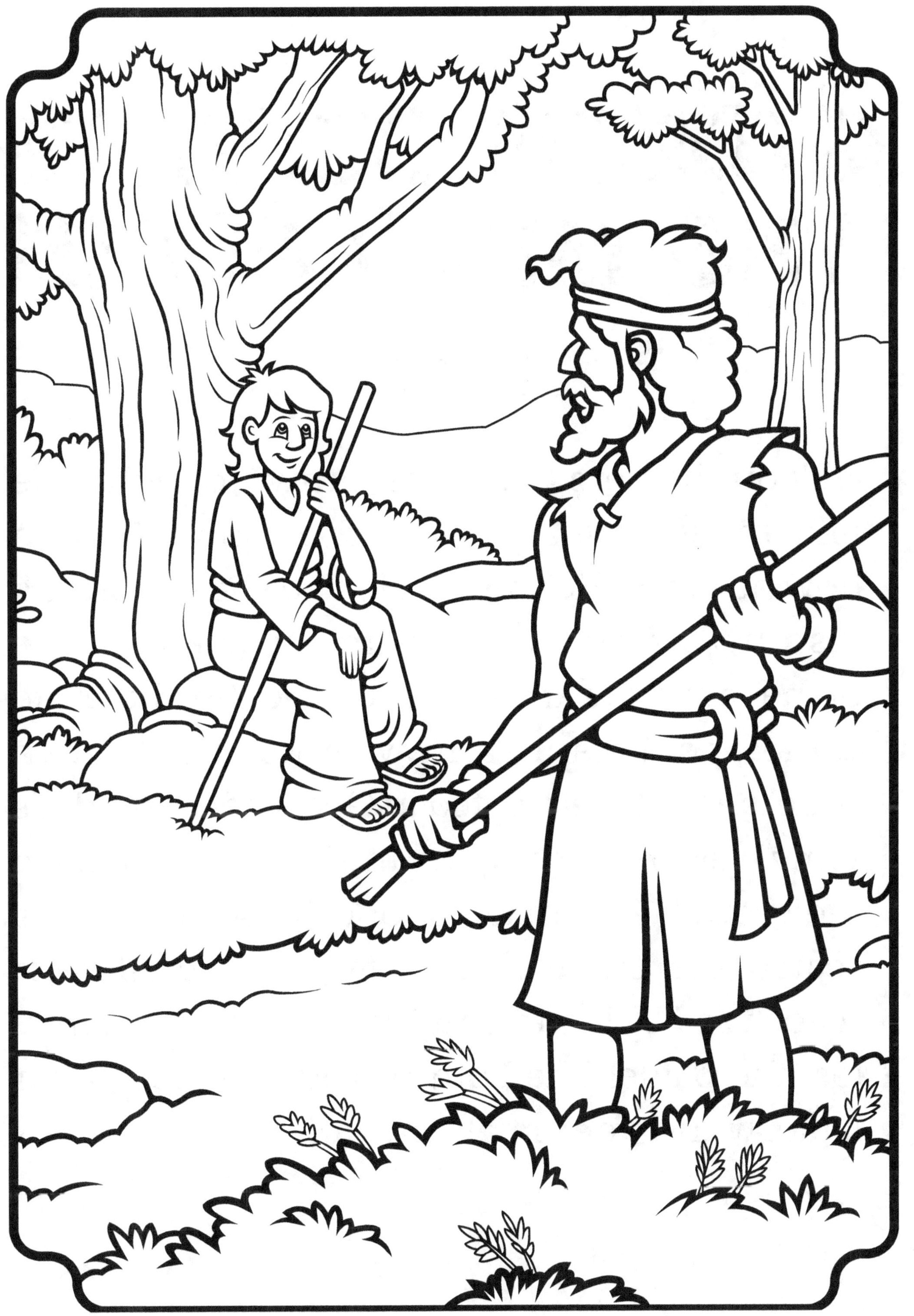

GIDEON DEFEATS THE MIDIANITES

JUDGES 7

Gideon gathered a large army to fight the Midianites. But God wanted to show Gideon how powerful He was, so He had Gideon shrink his army down to a small number. In the middle of the night, the army surrounded the Midianite camp. The Midianite army was much larger than Israel's. But Israel trusted in God. Gideon and his army blew their trumpets and broke their jars on the ground and made a loud noise. The noise scared the enemy. Their fear and confusion made the Midianite army so confused that they lost the battle! The Lord provided a victory for Israel with a very small army of men.

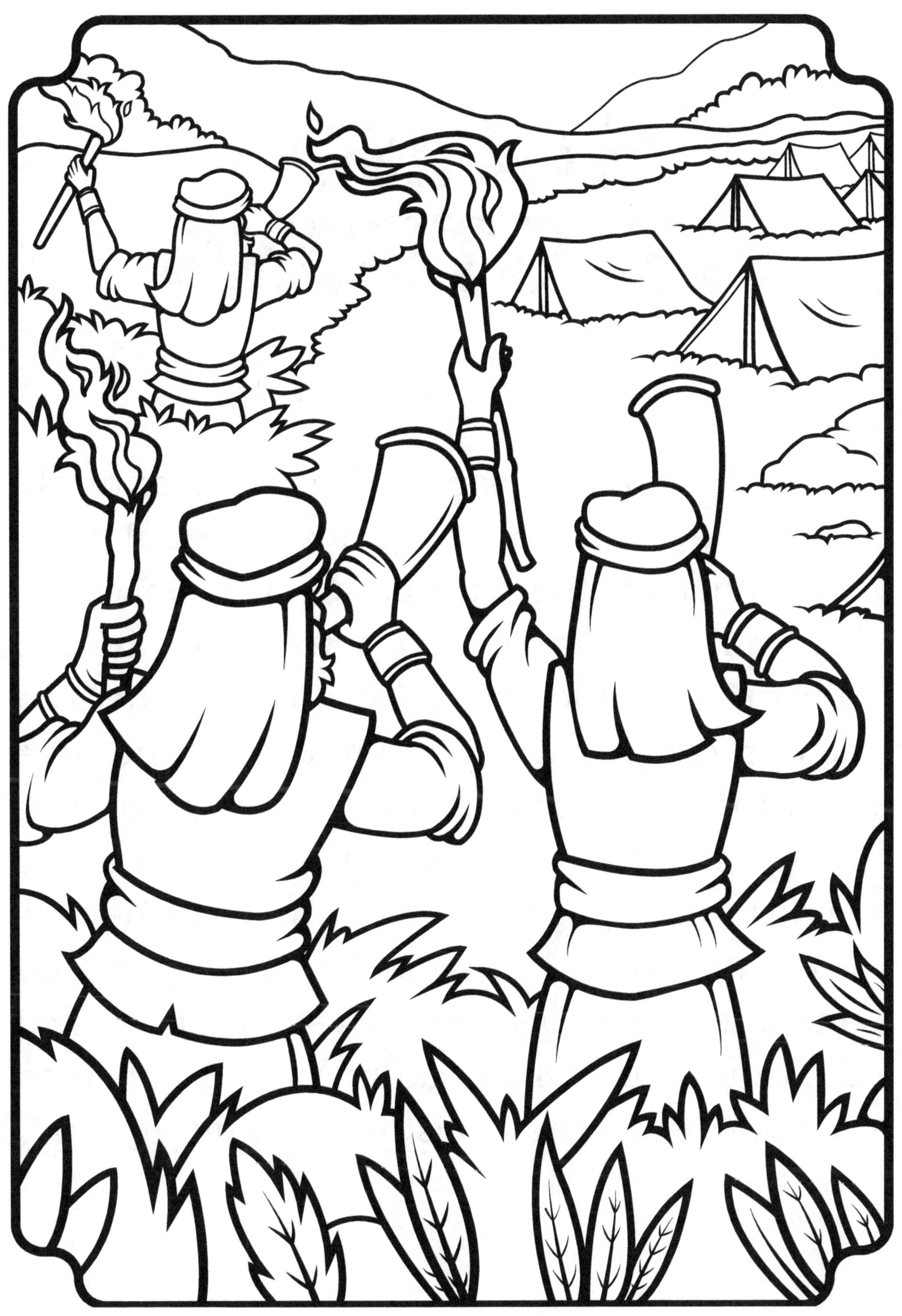

SAMSON IS STRONG

JUDGES 13-16

An angel came to Samson's parents and told them they were going to have a special baby. The angel told them the baby was never to cut his hair. After Samson was born, God helped him grow big and strong. He fought for the Lord against people named the Philistines who were very mean to God's people. One day, Samson let a woman named Delilah cut his hair. The Philistines captured Samson because he was no longer strong because he disobeyed God and cut his hair. God still loved and protected Samson, and while captured, God helped Samson defeat the Philistines and glorify God.

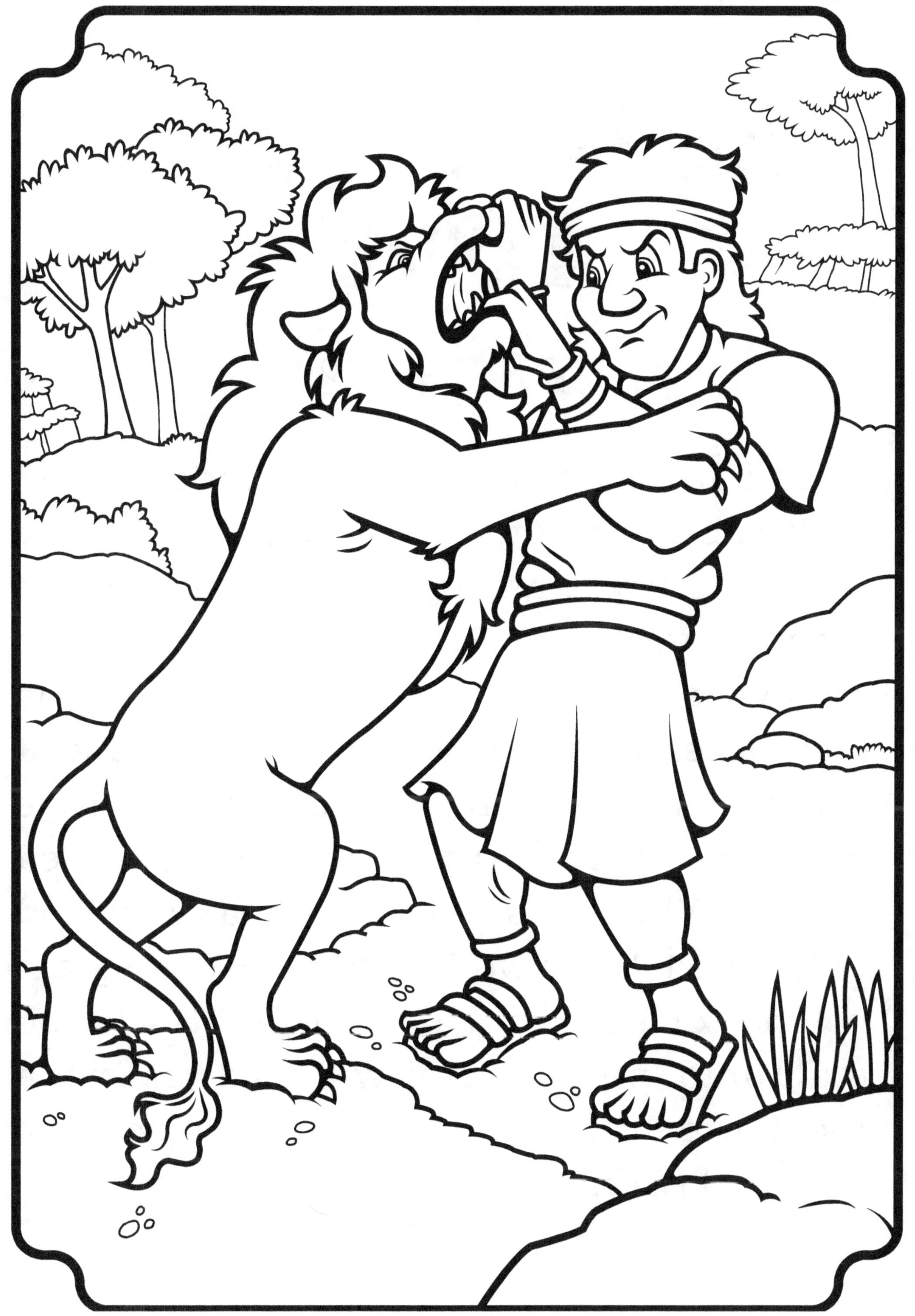

RUTH SHOWS LOVE

RUTH 1-2

Naomi and Ruth were very good friends and took care of each other. They did not have any money to buy anything to eat! They needed grain to make bread. Ruth went to a field where men were gathering grain. She picked up the little pieces the men dropped and left behind. It was very hard work. But she did it because she loved her friend. A man named Boaz owned the field. When he saw Ruth, he was very kind to her. He told his workers to leave extra grain behind for Ruth to gather. Naomi made the grain into bread. Naomi was glad to have a friend like Ruth to help her. God took care of Ruth and Naomi through love and friendship.

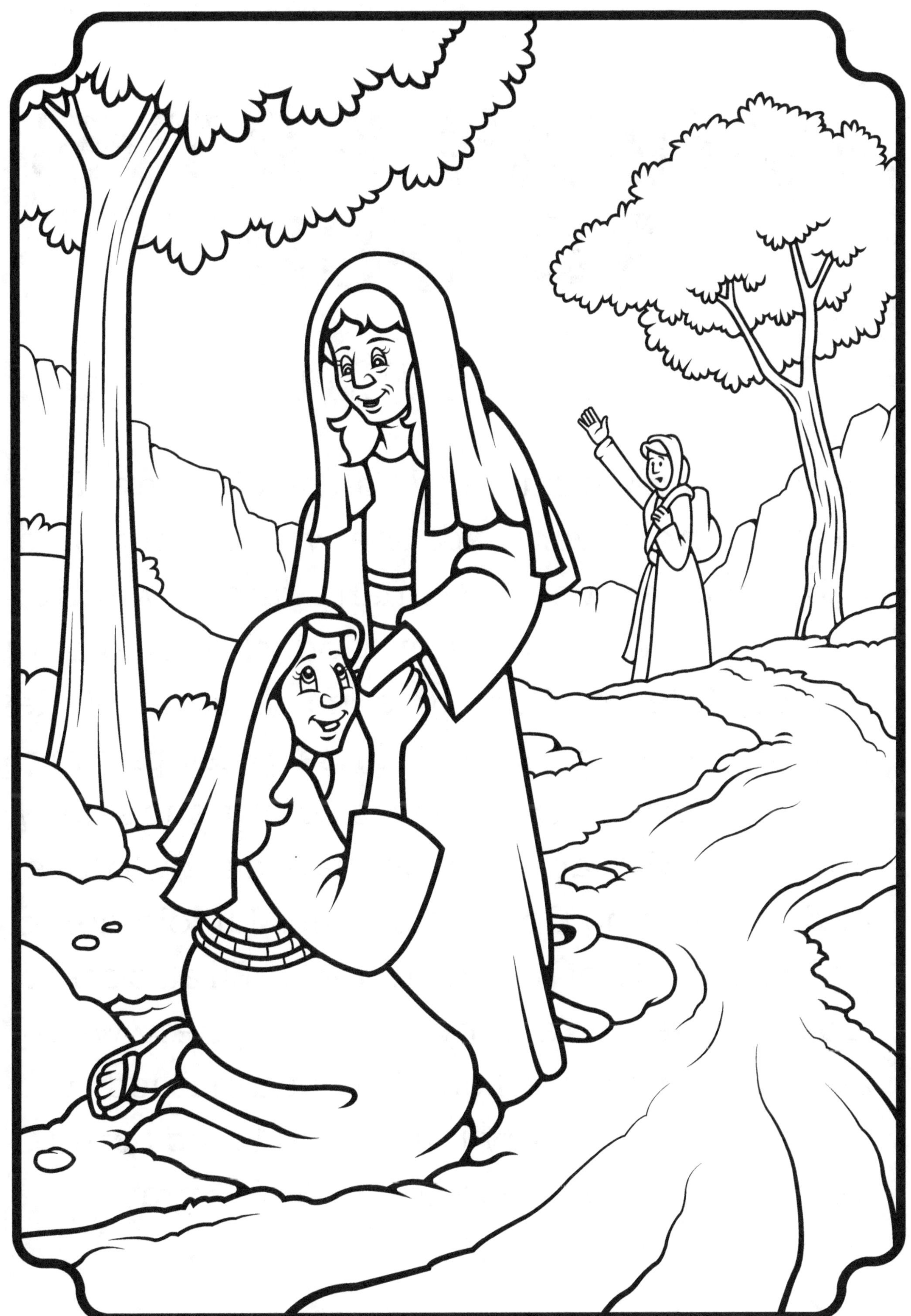

HANNAH PRAYS TO GOD

1 SAMUEL 1

Hannah and her husband had no children. This made Hannah very sad. She wanted to have a baby to love. When Hannah's family went to the Tabernacle to worship God, she cried and prayed, "Please, God, give me a son." While praying, a priest named Eli saw her praying. When he asked her what was wrong, she said, "I am very sad because I do not have a baby to love, and I am asking God to help me." Eli told her to go home and not be sad anymore. Eli also asked God to give her a baby boy and guess what? She gave birth to a baby boy and named him Samuel! She was very happy and loved Samuel very much. God answered Hannah's prayer.

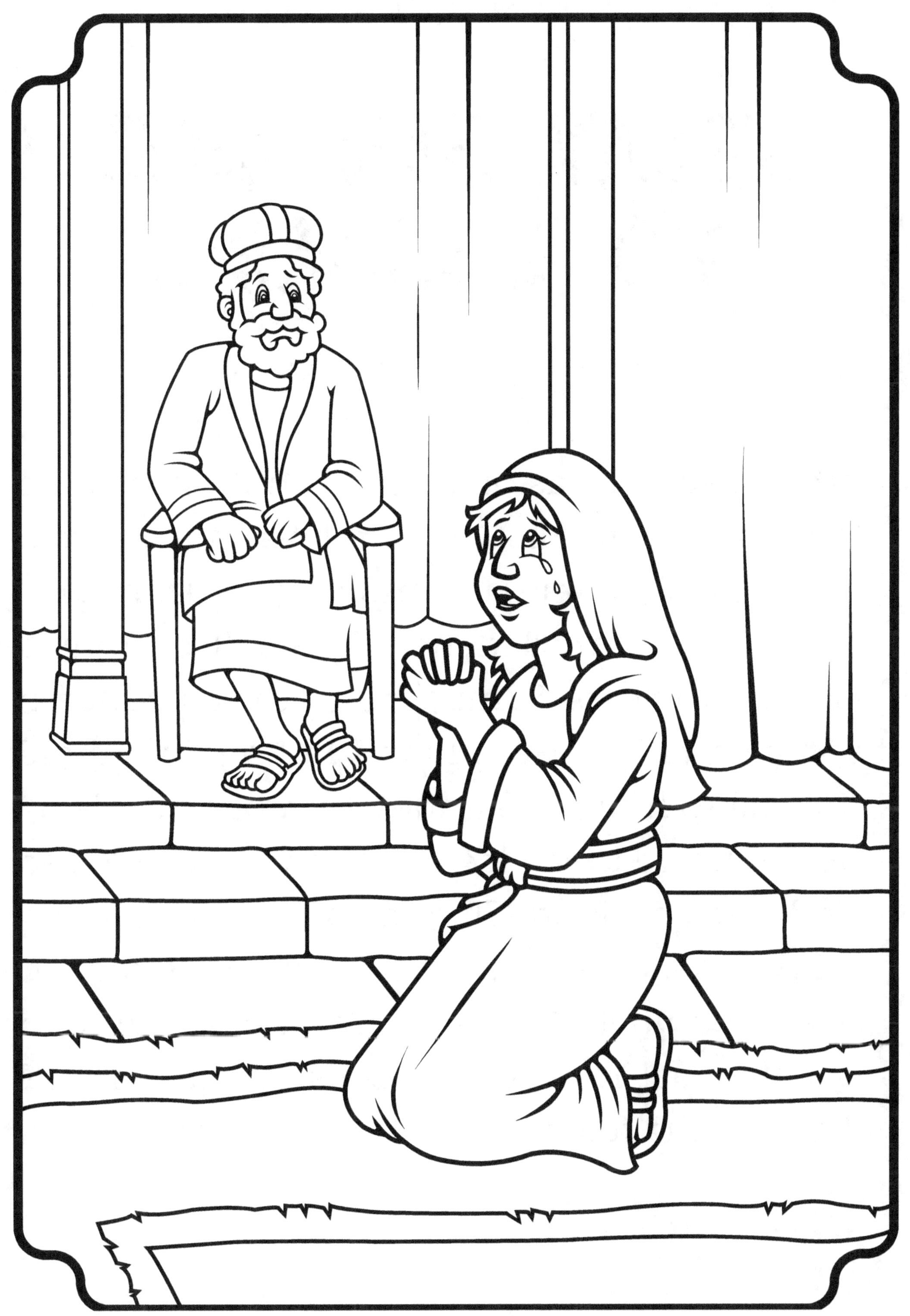

GOD SPEAKS TO SAMUEL

1 SAMUEL 3

When Samuel was older, he went to live at the tabernacle with Eli. One night, Samuel heard a voice say, "Samuel!" He jumped up and ran to Eli. "Here I am. You called me." Eli said, "No, I didn't. Go back to sleep!" Samuel heard the voice again and said to Eli, "Here I am!" But again, Eli did not call to him! So Samuel went back to sleep. But he heard the voice a third time. Eli realized God was speaking. Eli told Samuel what to do if it happened again. So Samuel went back to sleep. "Samuel!" God said. Samuel sat up and said, "Speak! Your servant is listening!" Samuel listened and followed God's directions.

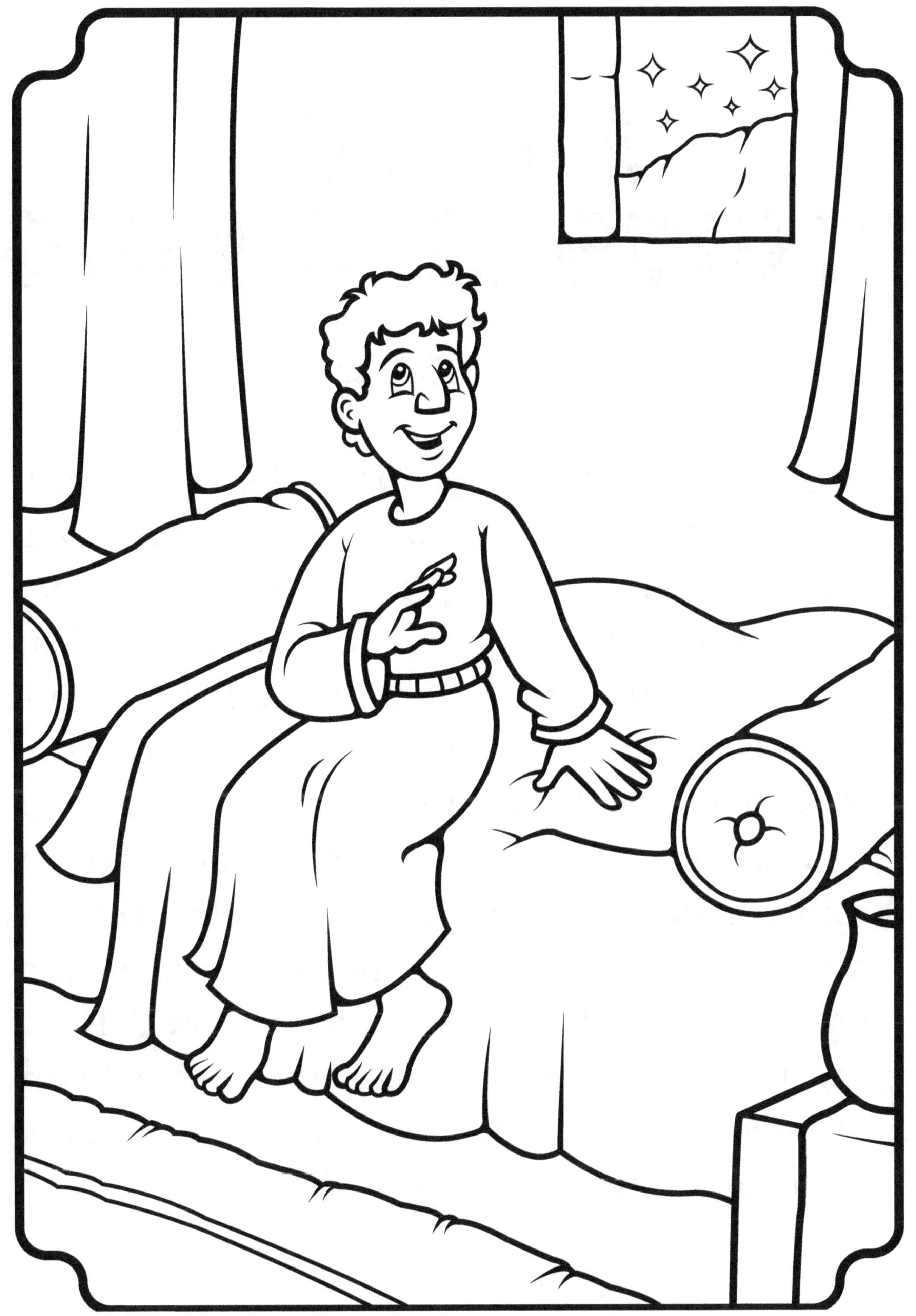

SAMUEL CHOOSES A KING

1 SAMUEL 9-10

Samuel grew up loving God and serving Him. He became the leader of Israel. Samuel was getting old, and the people said to Samuel, "Give us a king!" Samuel prayed to God about what to do. A man named Saul was looking for his father's lost donkeys. As Saul walked into town, God told Samuel, "That man is the one I want to be king." God was talking about Saul. Samuel said to Saul, "Come with me." Samuel poured oil on Saul's head and said, "The Lord has chosen you to be the king of His people, Israel." Then Samuel helped Saul learn all he needed to learn to become king. God chose Saul to be king. Samuel helped Saul.

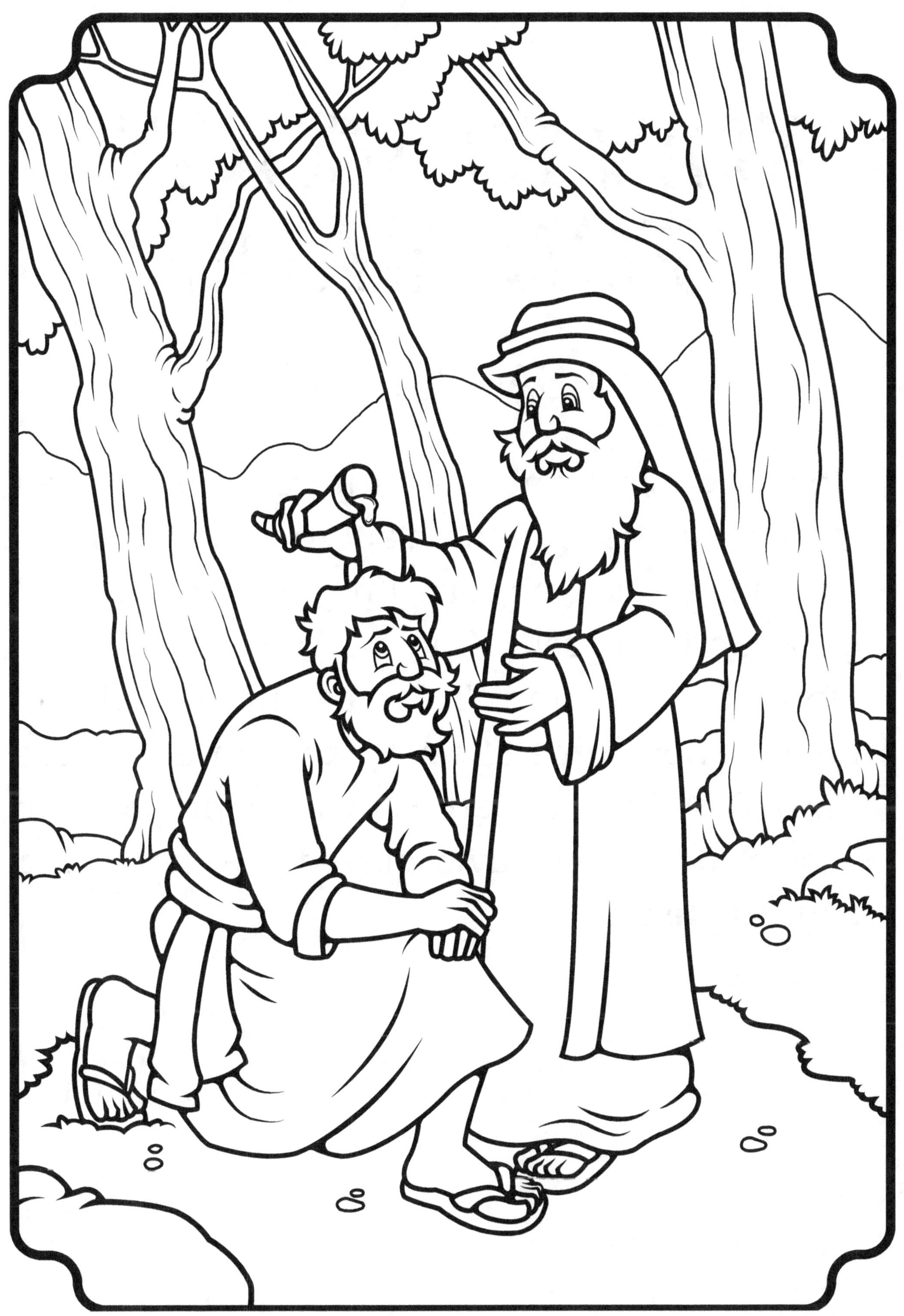

DAVID PLAYS FOR SAUL

1 SAMUEL 16

God's people wanted a king. Samuel prayed to God, and God chose Saul to be king of His people, Israel. One day, King Saul didn't feel good and was sad. King Saul's servants were worried about him. To make King Saul feel better, a boy named David played music on his harp. David loved God. He was happy to help King Saul. When David played the harp, King Saul felt better.

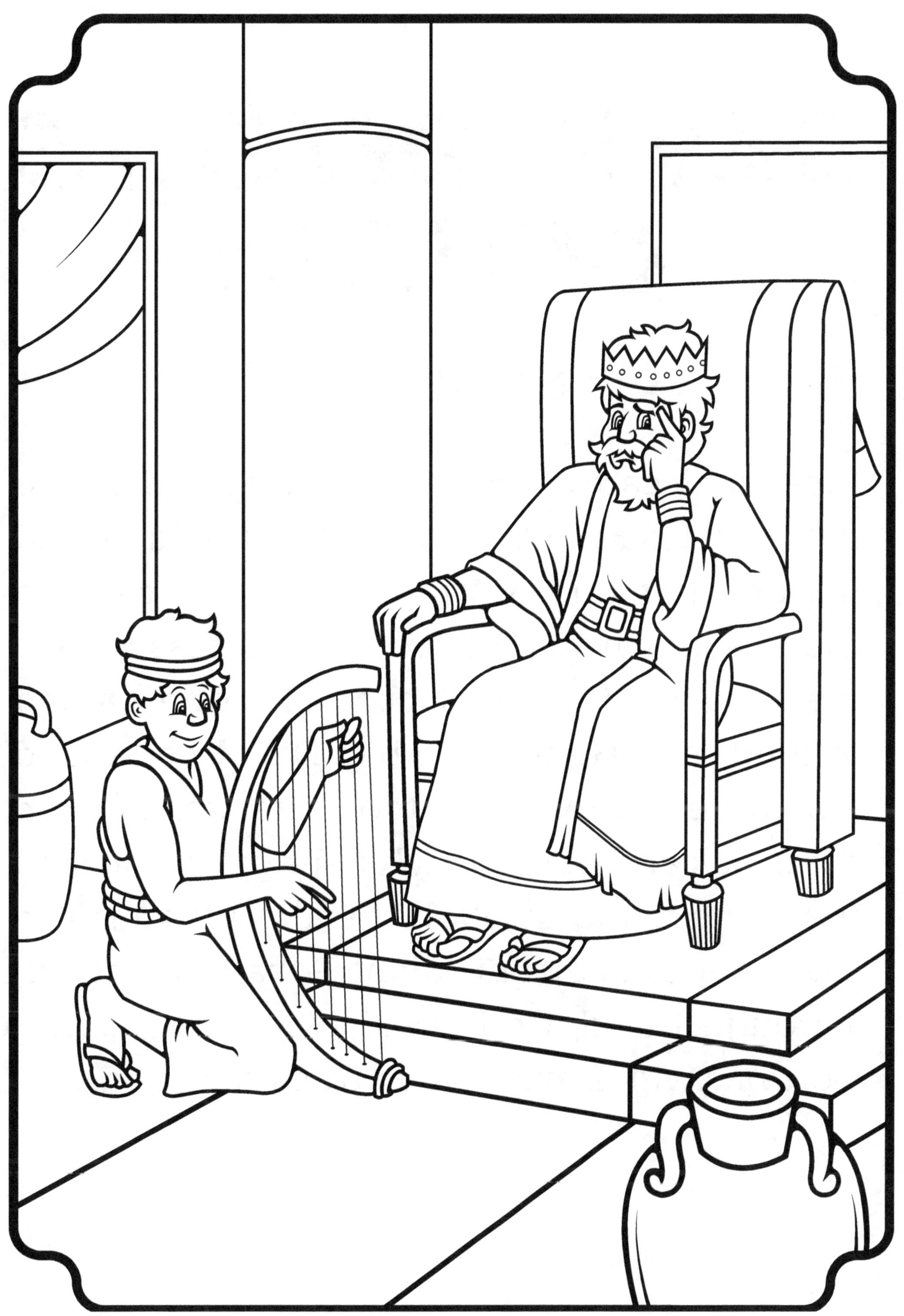

DAVID DEFEATS GOLIATH

1 SAMUEL 17

David took care of his father's sheep and played the harp for King Saul. One day, David visited his brothers and King Saul. They were with the Israelite army and were being teased by a great big giant named Goliath. No one wanted to fight him. He was too big. David knew God would help him, so he took five stones from the brook and put one in his slingshot. He sent the stone flying through the air. "Wham!" The stone knocked that big giant Goliath right over! Through David, God saved his people, Israel. God was with David. David trusted in God.

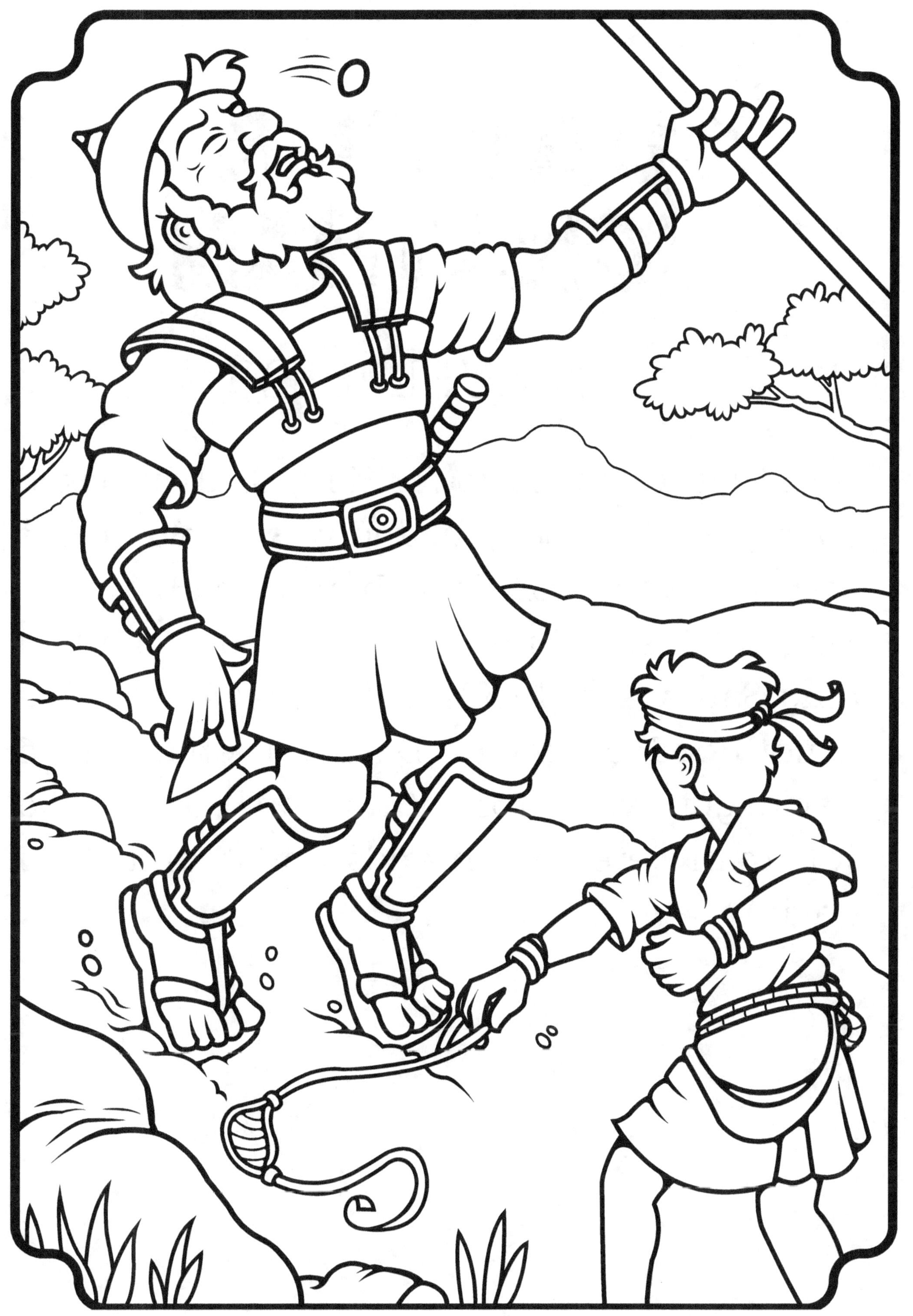

DAVID & JONATHAN

1 SAMUEL 18-20

David played his harp for King Saul, knocked down the giant Goliath, and was a soldier. His friend's name was Jonathan. Jonathan was King Saul's son! One day, David found out that King Saul wanted to hurt David! Oh no! That is not good! Jonathan, David's friend, helped David get away from King Saul. David and Jonathan were good friends. Jonathan helped David.

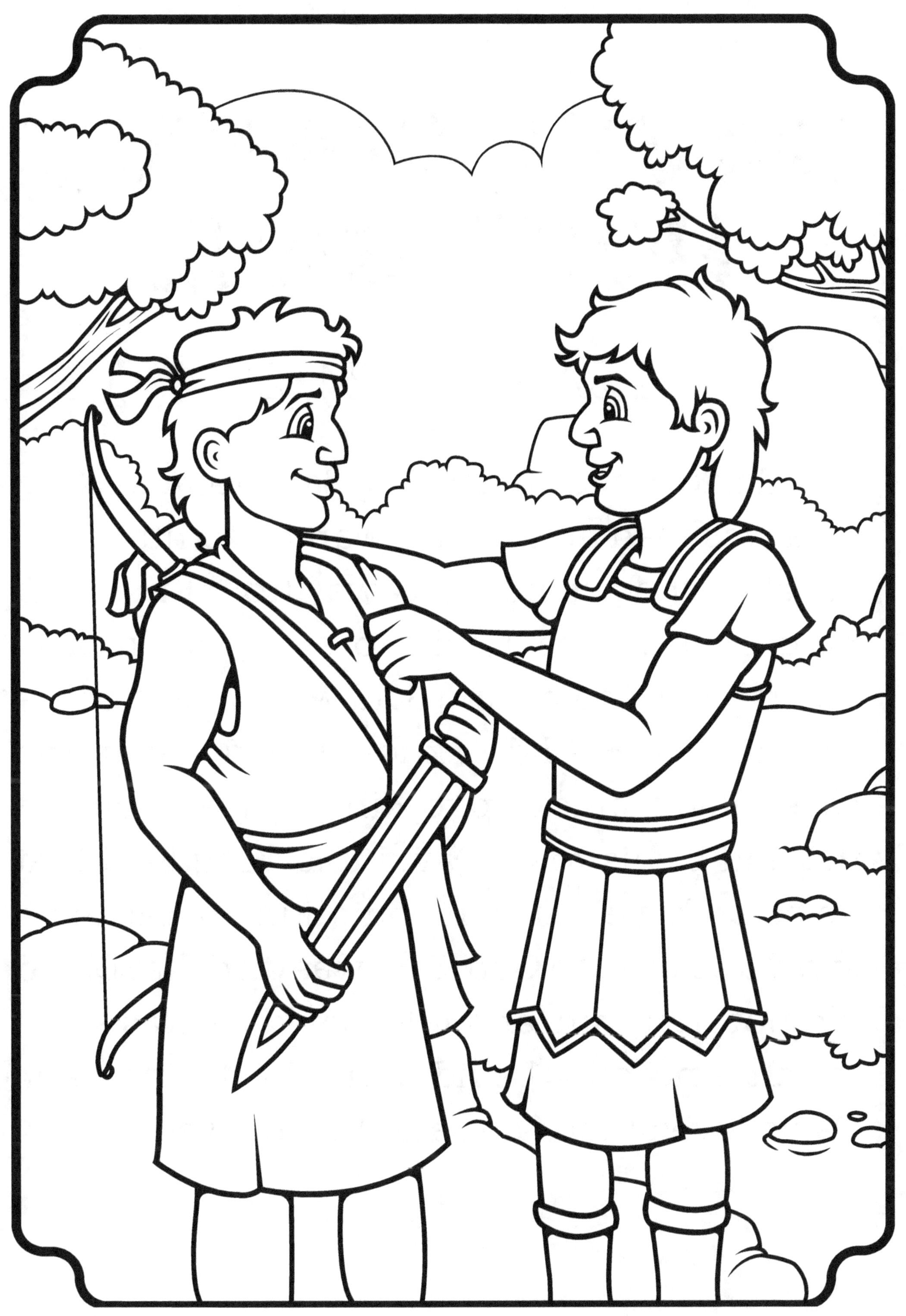

DAVID DOESN'T HURT SAUL

1 SAMUEL 24, 26

David had to hide from King Saul because King Saul was mad at him and wanted to hurt him. Jonathan helped him get away from King Saul. King Saul chased David to a big, dark cave. David hid in there. King Saul went inside of the cave to rest. He didn't know David was in the cave! David snuck up to King Saul and cut off the end of his robe. David told King Saul that he could have hurt him, but didn't because he loved and obeyed God. Saul was glad that David did not hurt him, and told David he was sorry for chasing him. David didn't hurt King Saul. David loved King Saul, and David loved God.

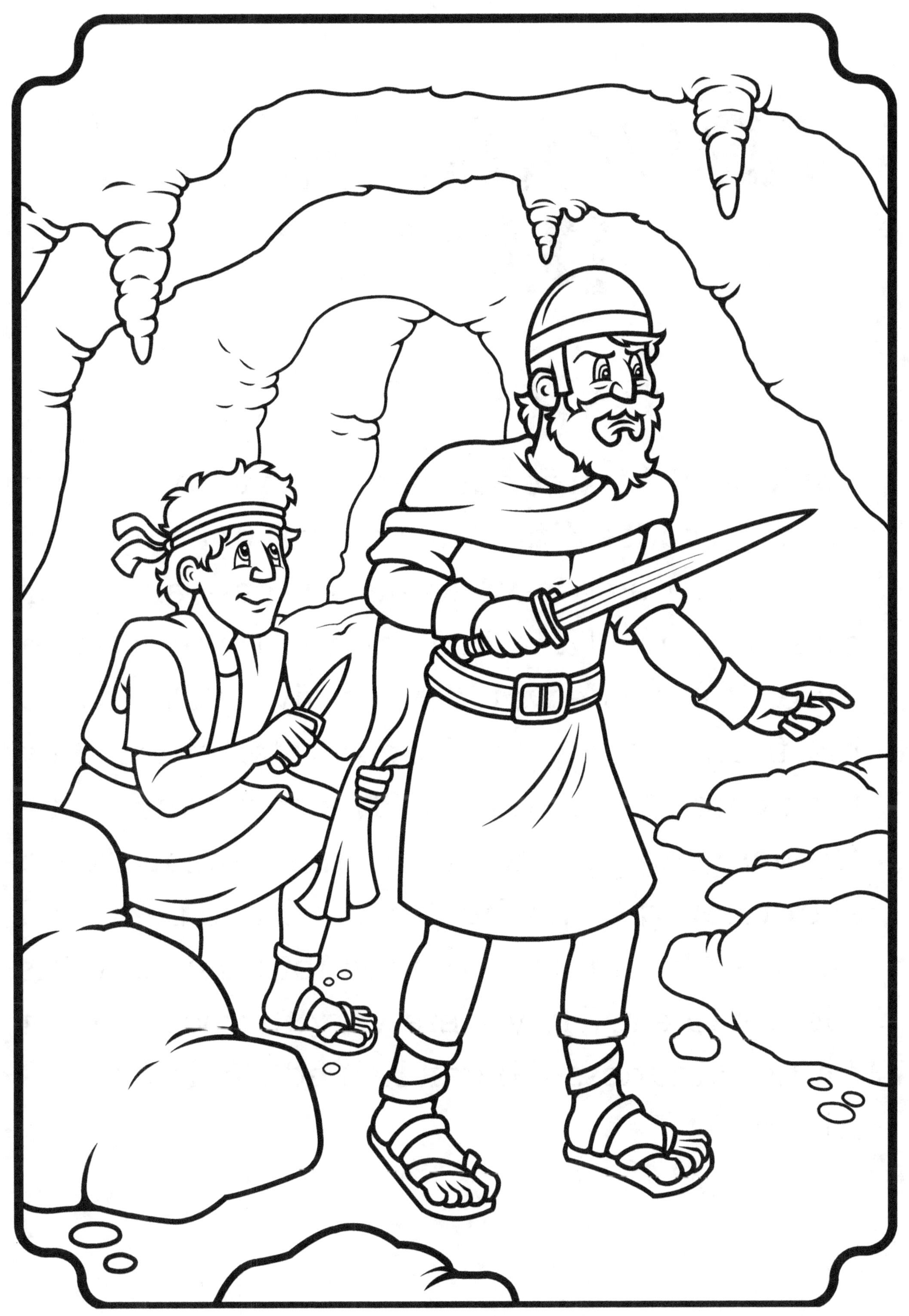

ABIGAIL HELPS DAVID

1 SAMUEL 25

David and his friends had to live in the hot desert because King Saul was still chasing him! One day, David saw some animals and took care of them. He asked the man who owned the animals if he would mind giving David and his friends some food and water since they took care of his animals. The man said, "No!" He was grumpy. The man's wife, Abigail, heard about how grumpy her husband had been and gathered lots and lots of food for David and his friends to eat. They were very thankful to her for her kindness. Abigail helped David and his friends.

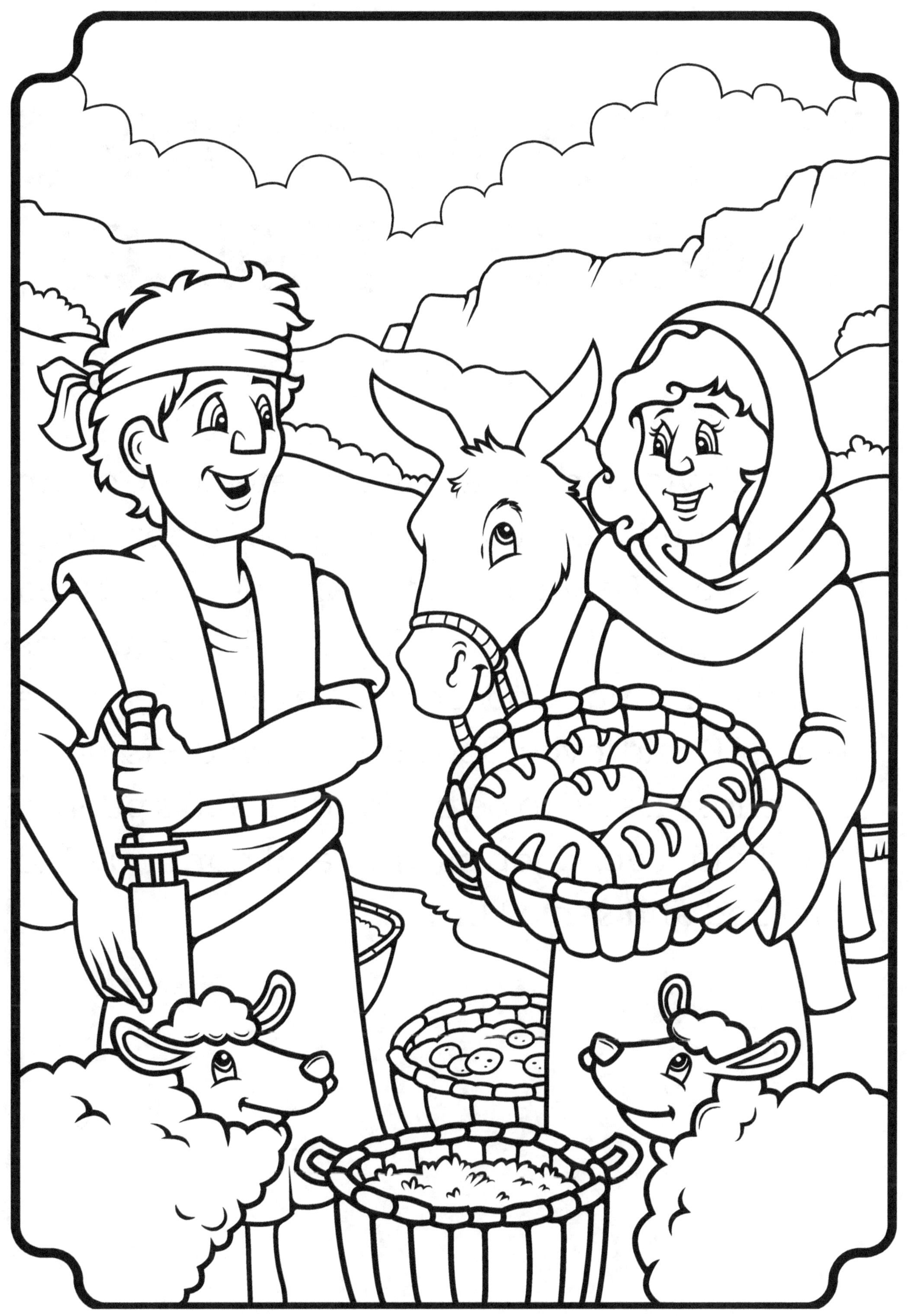

DAVID BECOMES KING OF ISRAEL

2 SAMUEL 5

When David was just a boy, he defeated Goliath with a slingshot! When he grew older, King Saul chased David out of the kingdom! But God had big plans for David. When King Saul was no longer king, God chose David to lead the people! David loved God and followed His word. God chose David to be the king of God's people. David did a good job as king and continued to love God and serve Him.

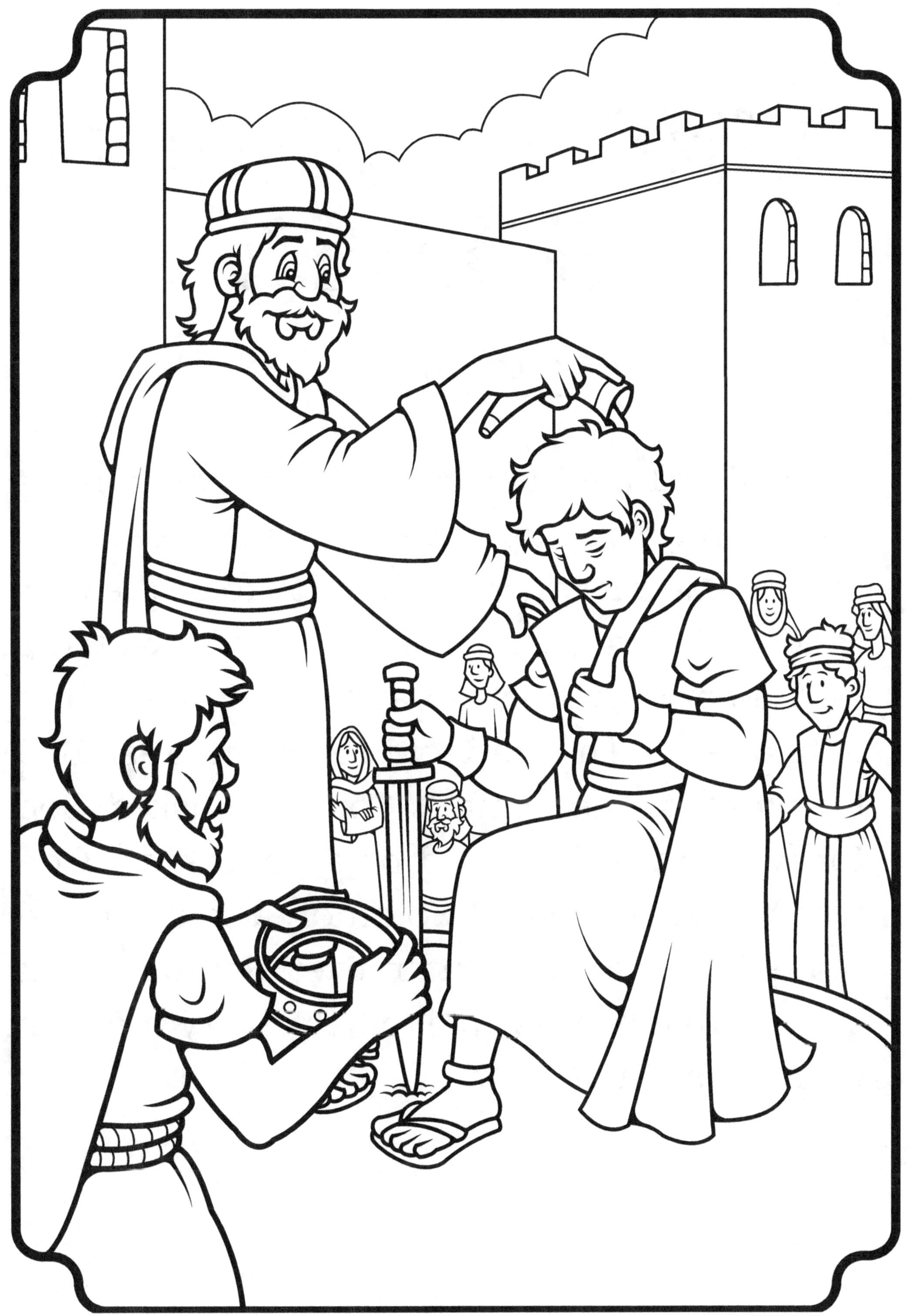

KING SOLOMON IS WISE

1 KINGS 3

When King David died, his son Solomon took his place. King Solomon loved God just like David did. He knew it would be a big job to be the new King, so he went to a special place to worship God. Solomon fell asleep, and God spoke to him in his dream. The Lord told Solomon to ask God for whatever he wanted. Solomon asked God for wisdom so he could be a good king. God was happy with what Solomon asked for and made him the wisest man ever! Solomon was so wise that he was able to help everyone with their problems.

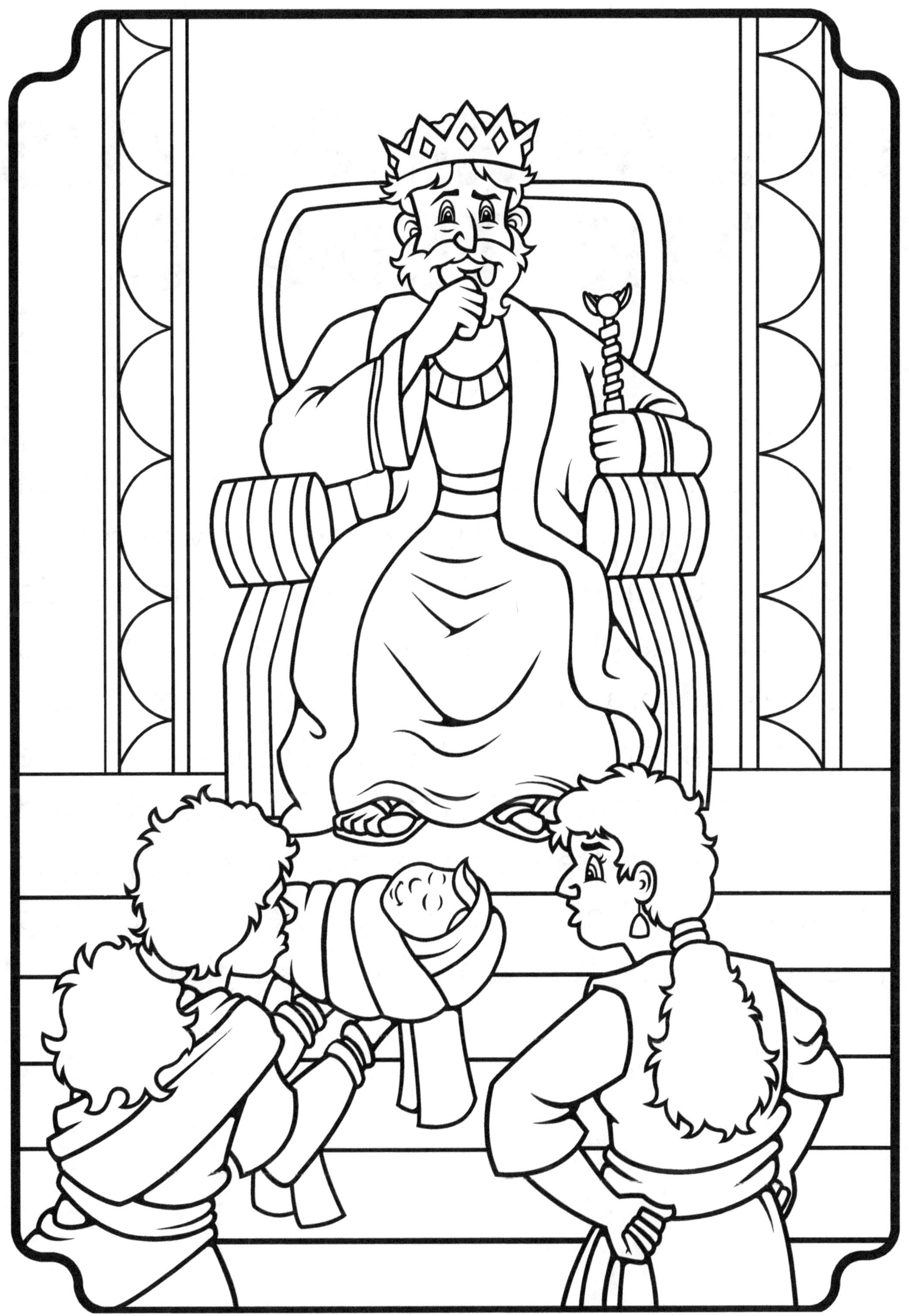

SOLOMON BUILDS THE TEMPLE

1 KINGS 6-8

King Solomon was very wise and did a lot of good things for God's people. He wanted to build a temple for God. The temple would be a special place for the people of Israel to come and pray to God and learn about Him. A lot of people helped King Solomon. There were many beautiful things in the temple, and everything glittered with gold! God's people worked together to build a temple for God. King Solomon was their king. He was a good king.

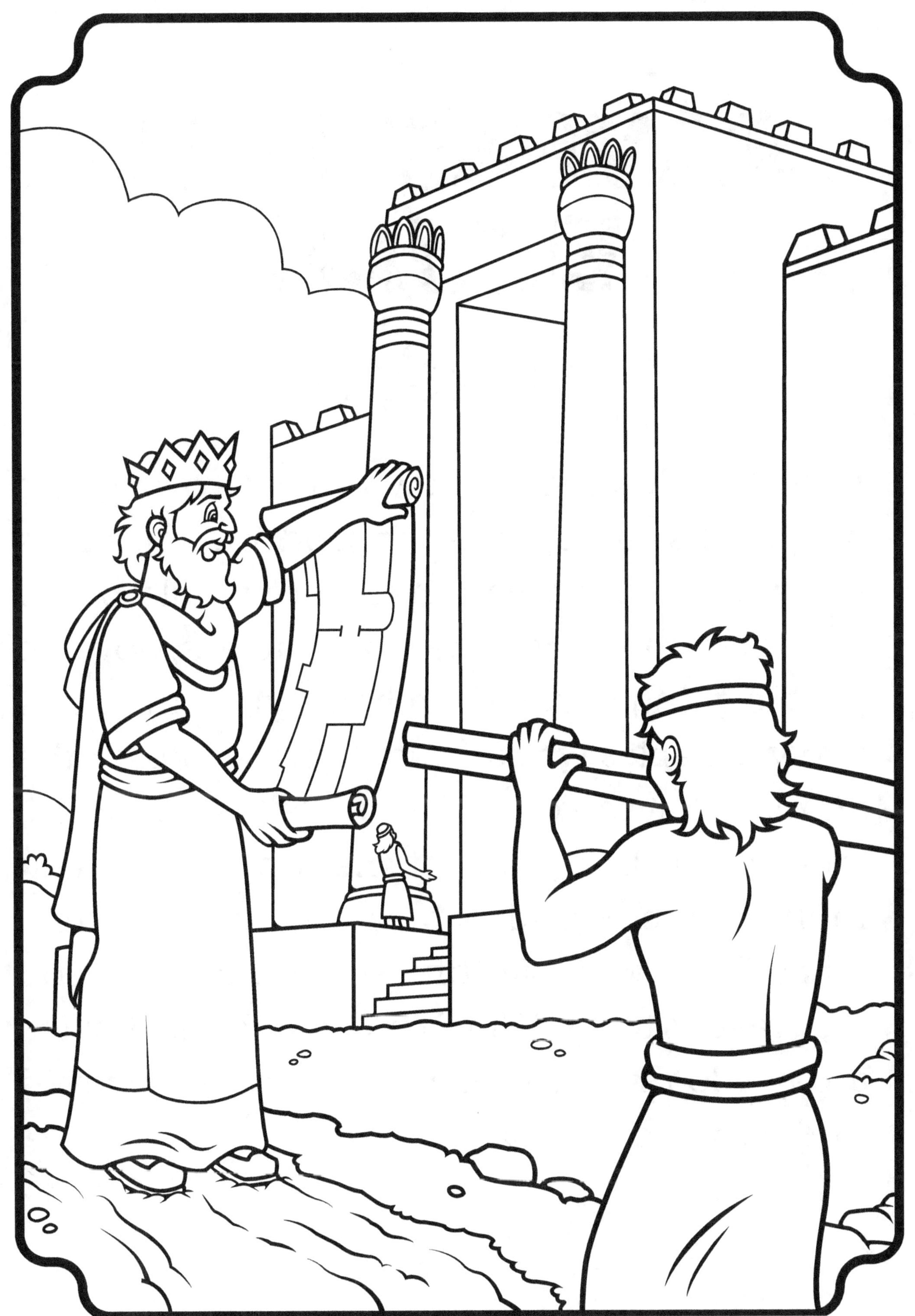

RAVENS FEED ELIJAH

1 KINGS 17

After King Solomon, a new king was over God's people. His name was Ahab. God told one of his servants named Elijah that there would be no rain for a long, long time! Without rain, how are people going to eat? Rain helps grow the fruits and vegetables we eat, and it gives water to the animals that serve us. This made the king mad, and he ran Elijah out of the kingdom. Elijah found a brook with water and stayed there. Since Elijah was a faithful servant of God, God sent ravens to feed Elijah meat and bread twice a day. God helped Elijah because he obeyed God. Elijah loved God.

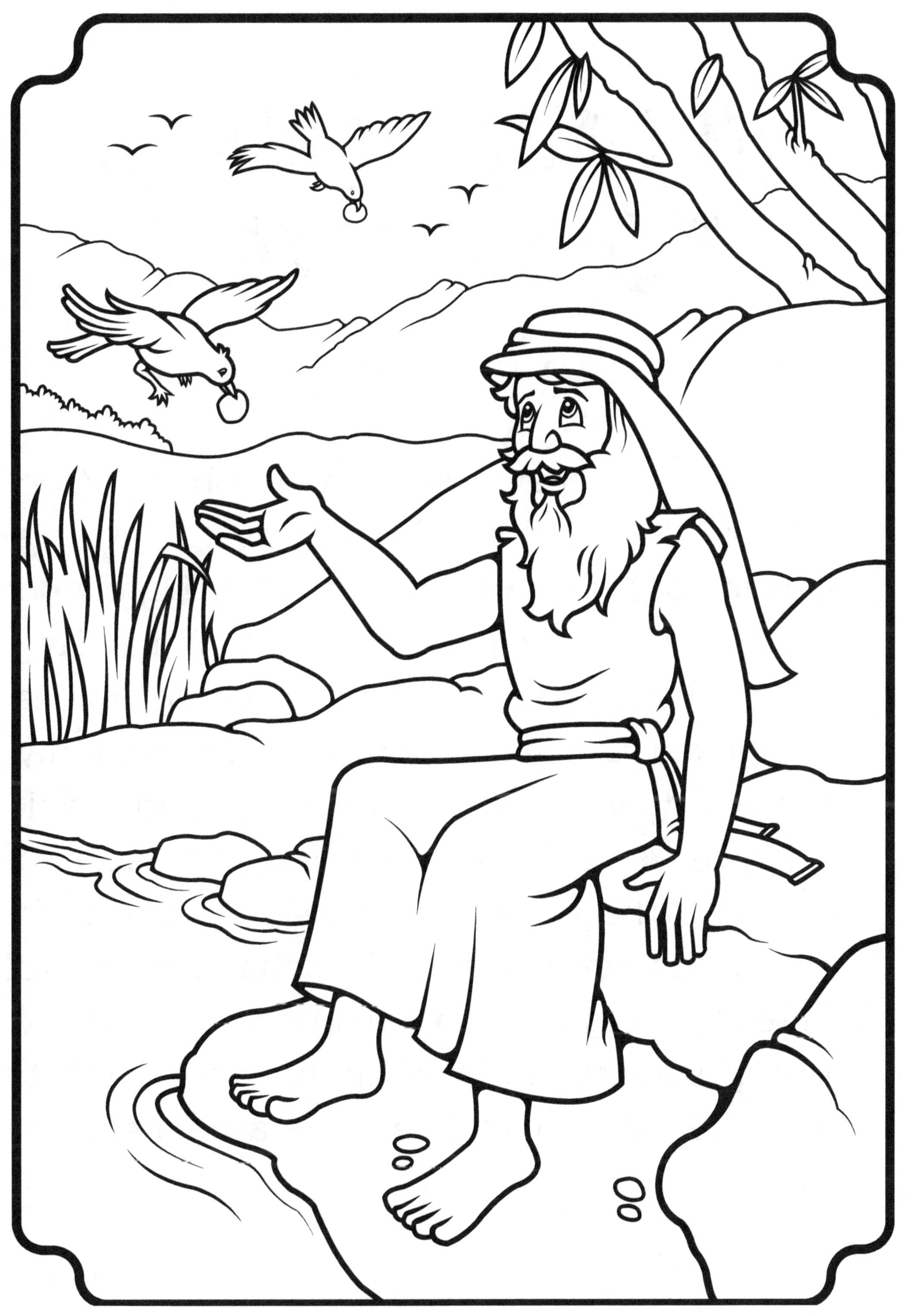

ELiJAH GOES TO HEAVEN

2 KINGS 2

Elijah was a special prophet who obeyed God and served Him. When Elijah was old, he was ready to go to heaven to be with God. Elijah and his friend Elisha walked by a river. While they were talking, a special chariot pulled by horses that looked like they were on fire suddenly swooped down and picked up Elijah and took him to heaven to be with God! This made Elijah very happy because he was ready to live with God in heaven! His friend Elisha was sad to see his friend go to heaven, but he was happy to keep serving God just as his friend Elijah had done. Like Elijah, Elisha became a special prophet.

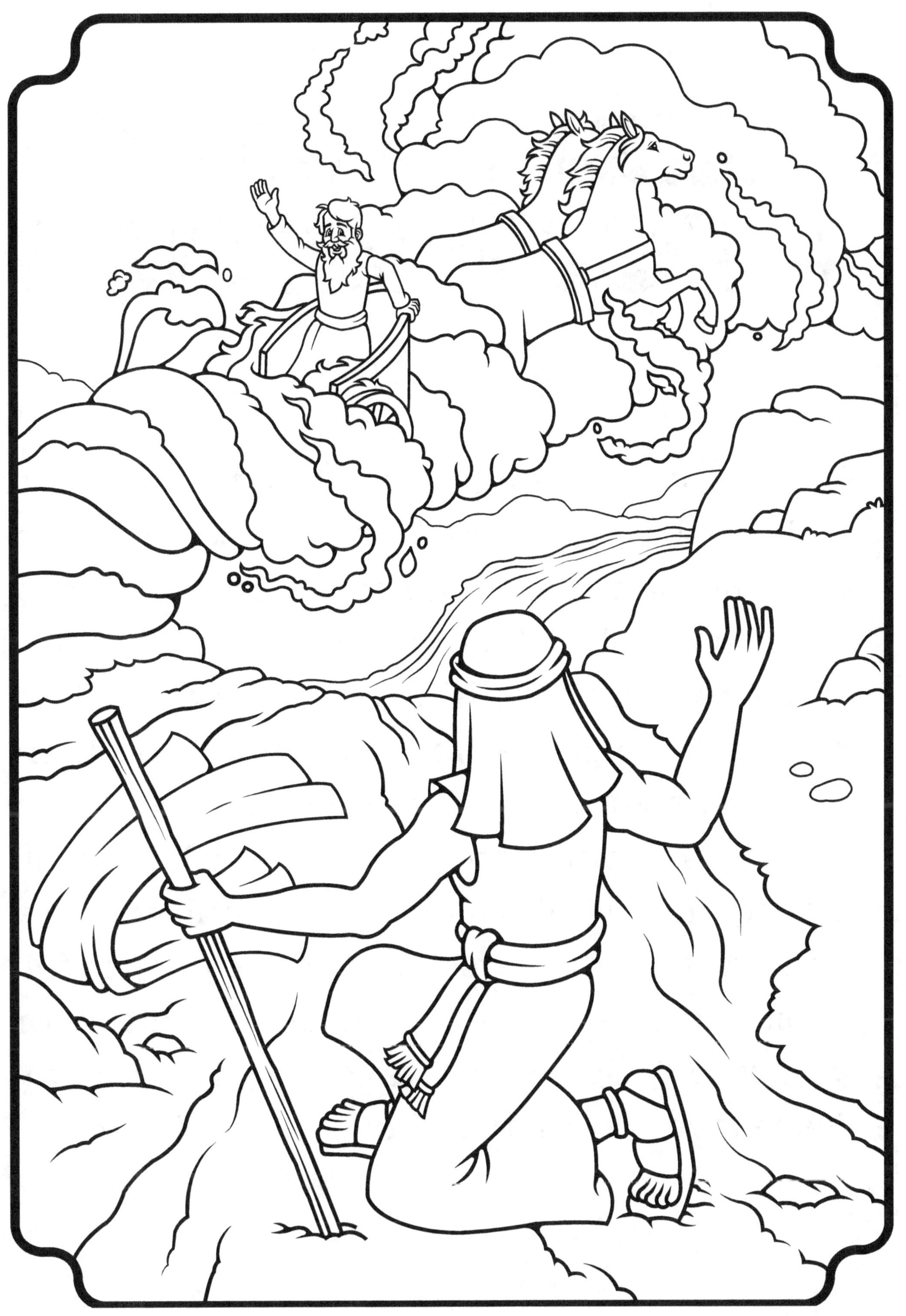

ELISHA HELPS A POOR WOMAN

2 KINGS 4

Elijah went to heaven in a chariot of fire, and Elisha took his place as a prophet. A poor woman asked Elisha for help one day because she had no money to buy food for herself or her sons. All she had was oil. Elisha told the poor woman to ask her neighbors for empty jars, and then fill the jars with the oil she had left. God then helped the woman by using her small jar to fill the big jars full of oil! Only God could make a small jar fill up big jars! She sold the big jars full of oil and made money! Elisha helped a poor woman out. God took care of the poor woman. Elisha loved and served God.

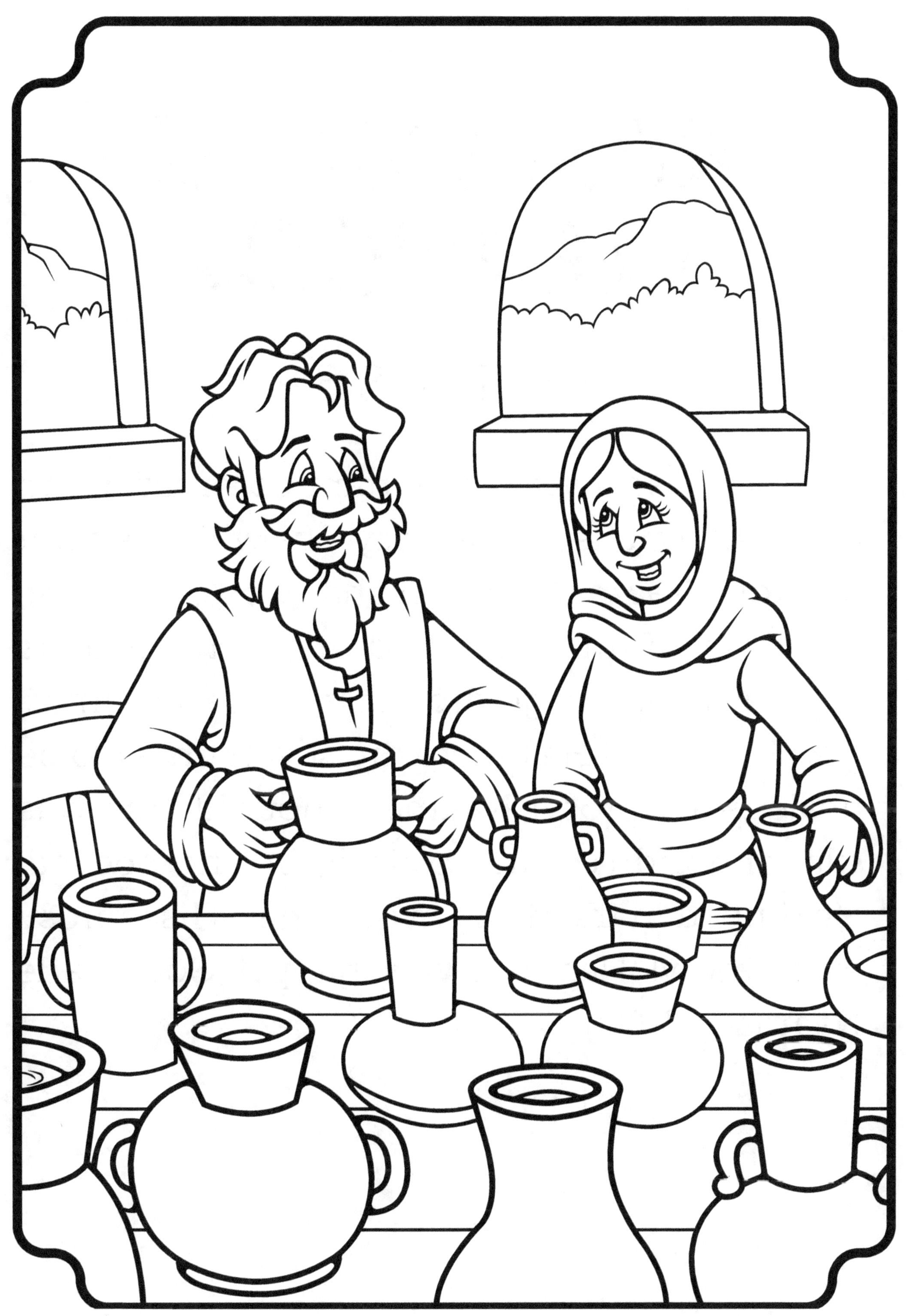

NAMAAN iS CLEANSED

2 KINGS 5

Naaman was a very important commander in the army, but he had leprosy. His wife's servant girl told Naaman that Elisha, God's prophet, could help him. Elisha told one of his helpers to tell Naaman to go dip in a river seven times. 1-2-3-4-5-6-7! He had to dip seven times to be healed of leprosy! Naaman thought this was silly and didn't want to do it, but he obeyed. He dipped in the river seven times. His leprosy went away! Naaman was happy! God made Naaman well!

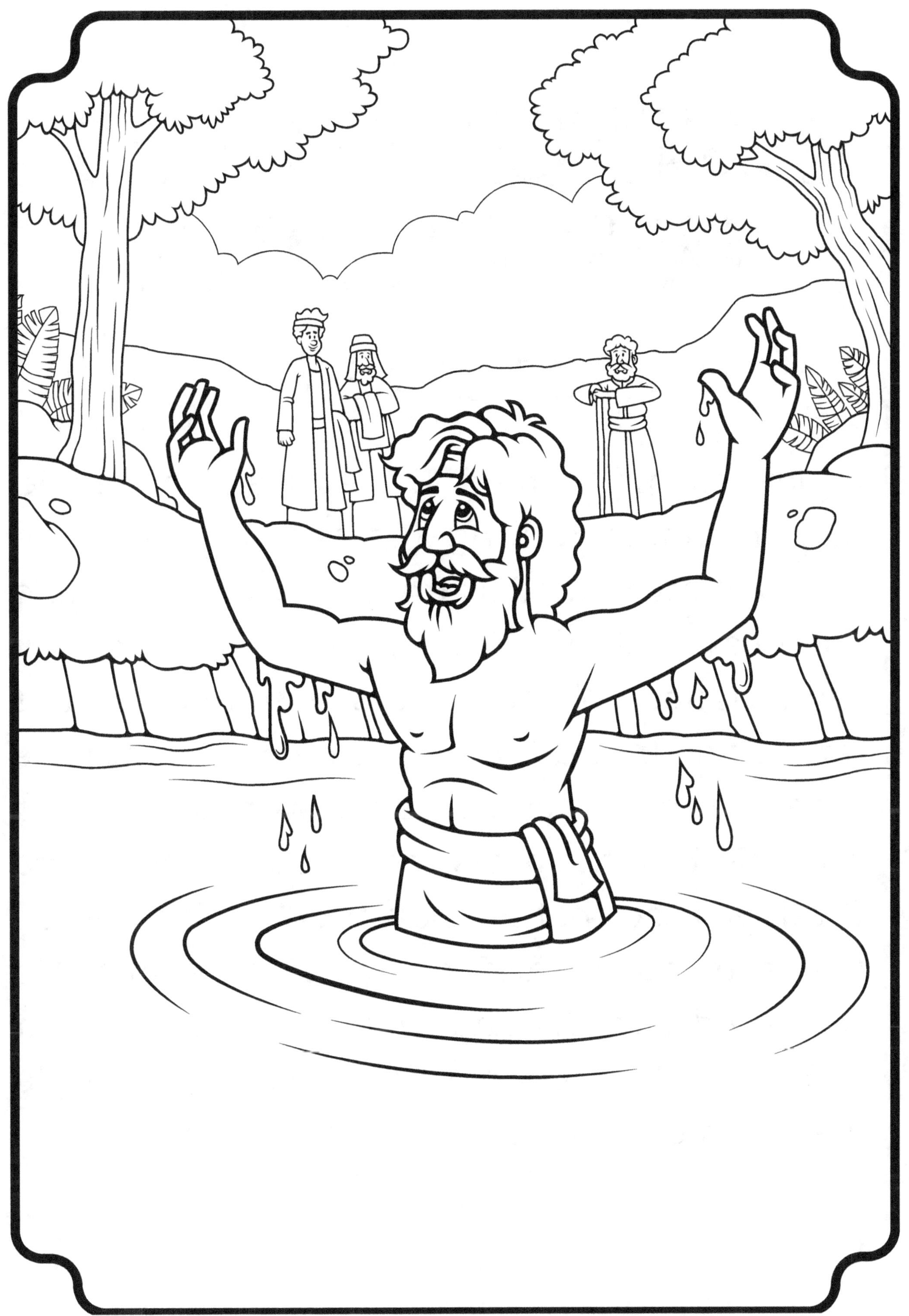

ESTHER SAVES HER PEOPLE

ESTHER 2-8

A Jewish girl named Esther was chosen to become queen to King Xerxes of Persia. There was a man named Haman who did not like Esther's people, the Jews. He wanted to destroy them. Queen Esther was sad scared for her family and friends when she heard of Haman's plan to hurt her people. Esther went to the King and told him the Jews were good people. The King was sad that Haman tried to destroy his beautiful queen and the Jewish people. He punished Haman and wrote a new law that protected God's people, the Jews. God's people were saved because Queen Esther was brave!

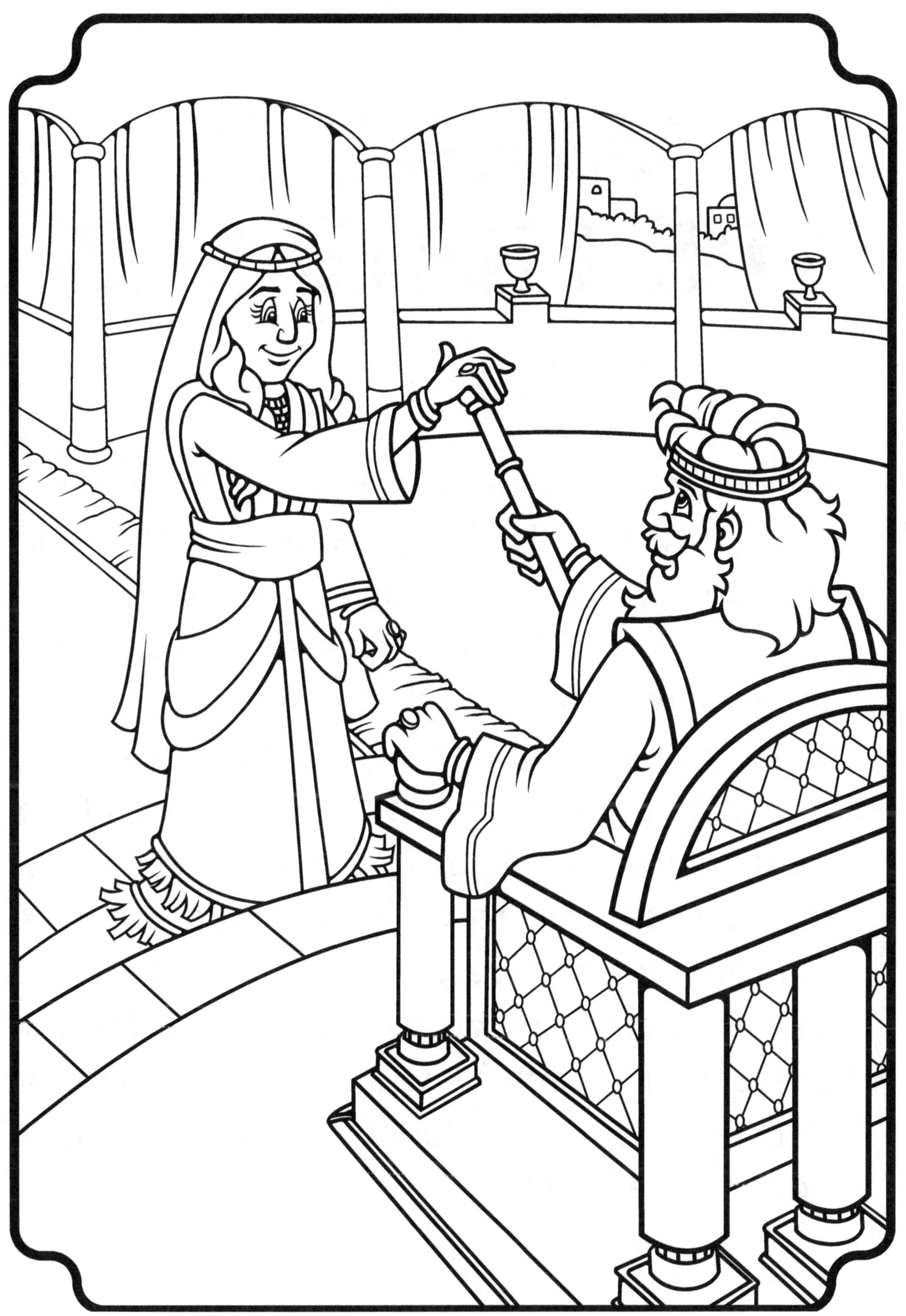

DANIEL & THE LIONS DEN

DANIEL 6

Daniel loved God and prayed to Him three times every day. The King made a rule that said the people should pray only to the King. Daniel did not follow this rule because he knew we should only pray to God. Daniel obeyed God. The King heard that Daniel did not pray to him, so he had Daniel thrown into a den of great big hungry lions! While in the lions den, Daniel continued to pray to God. The next day, the King came to see if Daniel was still alive and he was! God made sure the lions did not eat Daniel! The King told everyone what God had done for Daniel! Daniel loved God and prayed to Him. God protected Daniel.

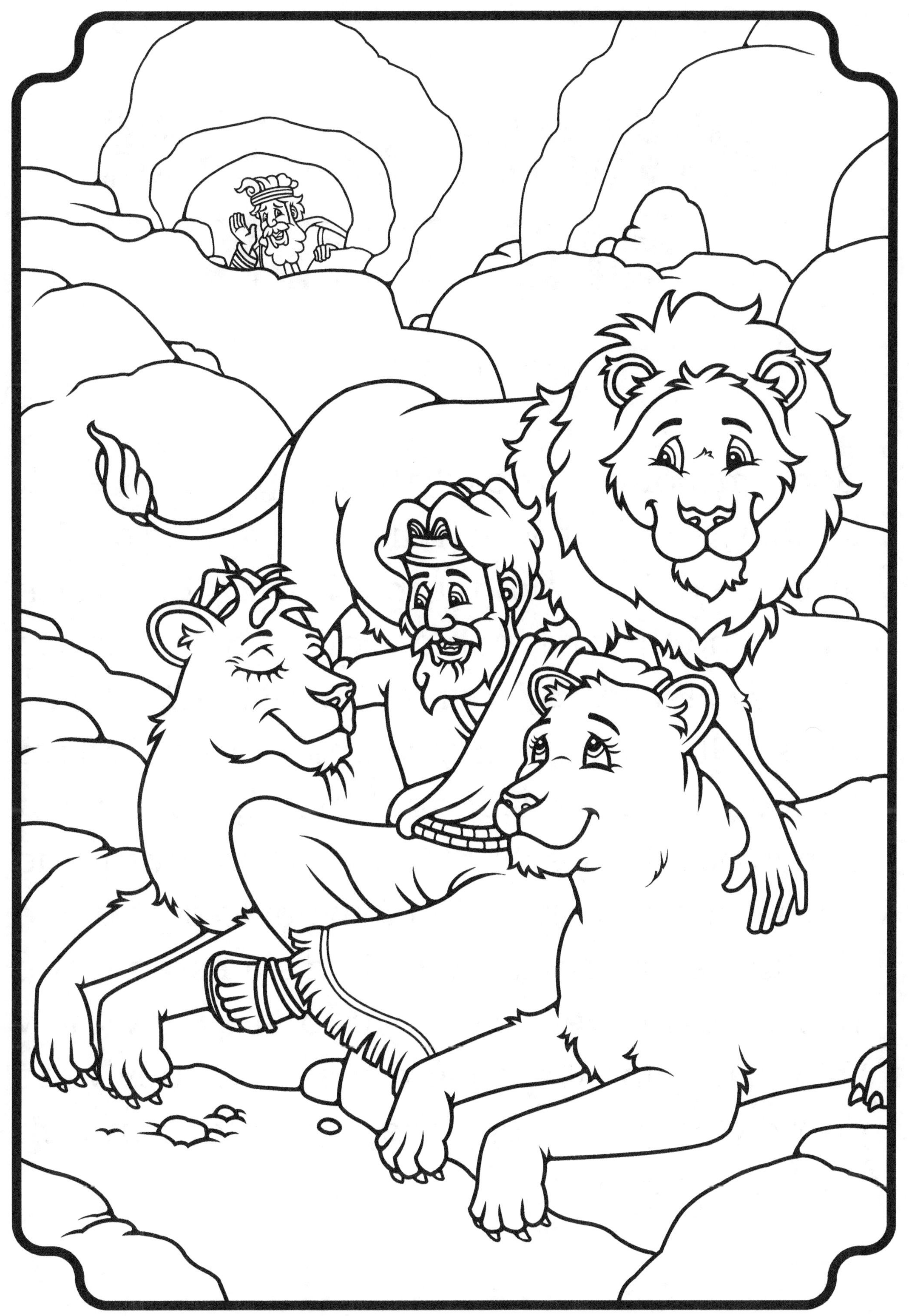

JONAH & THE BIG FISH

JONAH 1-3

God sent Jonah to go tell the people of Nineveh to obey God. But Jonah did not want to go! He disobeyed God and got in a boat. A big storm came and threw Jonah out of the boat! He was then swallowed by a great big fish and stayed in its belly for three days! Jonah asked God for a second chance. God told the big fish to spit Jonah out at Nineveh. Jonah was happy that he got a second chance! Jonah went to the people of Nineveh and told them God's message. The people of Nineveh listened to Jonah. They knew they had done wrong and they said they were sorry. God was happy the people of Nineveh listened to Him.

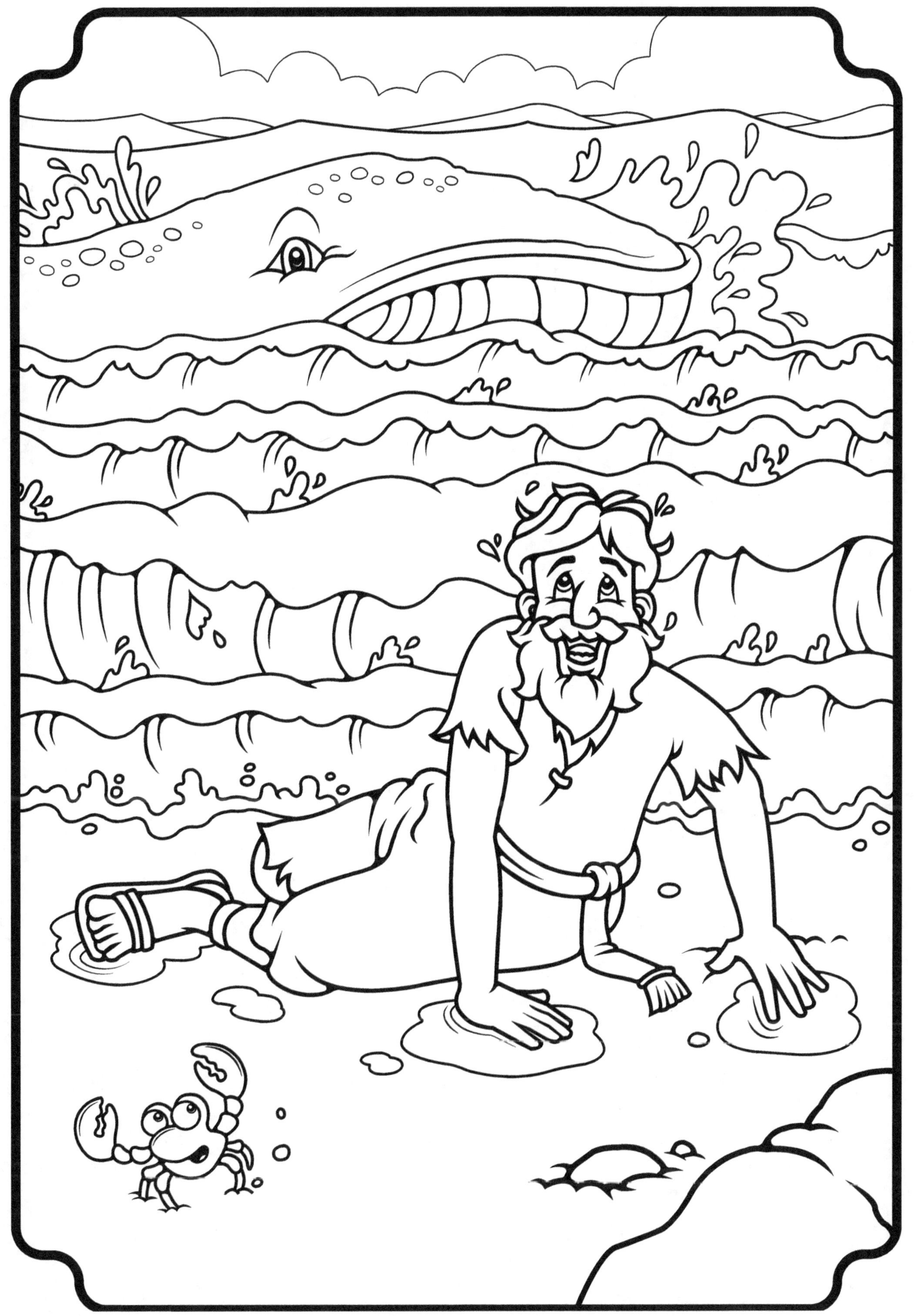